The one-day, limited-over cricket match has been one of the most revolutionary innovations made in cricket this century. Many of them have produced breath-taking finishes.

David Lemmon's book recalls some of the most memorable occasions from World Cup finals to League matches and includes two fascinating nostalgic accounts of one-day games played before the first limited-over competition in 1963.

For this paperback three accounts of 1983 matches have been included.

DAVID LEMMON is a Londoner whose interest in cricket began when he was first taken to Lord's during the war. He has been an enthusiast, collector and avid reader on the game ever since. He is a long-standing member of The Cricket Society, a speaker on the game throughout the country and a member of the Cricket Writer's Club. He was the pioneer editor of *Pelham Cricket Year*, first published in 1979, and is now the compiler of *Benson and Hedges Cricket Year*. He is the author or compiler of more than half a dozen other books on the game and is preparing a biography of Percy Chapman.

Great One-Day Cricket Matches

David Lemmon

London
UNWIN PAPERBACKS
Boston   Sydney

First published in Great Britain by Pelham Books Ltd, 1982
First published by Unwin Paperbacks, 1984

UNWIN ® PAPERBACKS
40 Museum Street, London WC1A 1LU, UK

Unwin Paperbacks
Park Lane, Hemel Hempstead, Herts HP2 4TE, UK

George Allen & Unwin Australia Pty Ltd
8 Napier Street, North Sydney, NSW 2060, Australia

British Library Cataloguing in Publication Data

Lemmon, David
    Great one-day cricket matches.
1. Cricket—History—20th century
I. Title
796.35'86   GV913
ISBN 0-04-796087-6

Printed in Great Britain
by Cox and Wyman Ltd,
Reading

*for Keith and Barry who
shared some of them with
me*

CONTENTS

LIST OF ILLUSTRATIONS

'The Old Brigade' takes the field for the one-day match at the Oval in May, 1946, to celebrate the centenary of the famous ground.

Ted Dexter holds the Gillette Cup as Sussex become the first winners.

Geoffrey Boycott has rarely batted better than in the 1965 Gillette Cup Final against Surrey.

West Indies captain, Clive Lloyd, hitting a huge six off Dennis Lillee during the 1975 Prudential World Cup final.

Basil D'Oliveira, the limping hero of a lost cause. Worcestershire v Kent, Benson and Hedges final, 1976.

Mike Procter bowling in the Benson and Hedges Hampshire v Gloucestershire match at Southampton, 1977.

Prudential World Cup final, 1979. Greenidge is run out by Randall.

Prudential World Cup final, 1979 — Collis King, Viv Richards and Joel Garner.

Benson and Hedges Cup final, 1979 — batting of the very highest quality from Graham Gooch and Ken McEwan.

Vincent van der Bijl, who was involved in a statistical oddity in the 1980 Benson and Hedges Cup match at Taunton.

The aggressive batting of Mike Gatting came close to bringing England victory in the 1981 Prudential Trophy match at Edgbaston.

Robin Jackman in buoyant mood after running out Trevor Chappell in a Prudential Trophy match.

NatWest final, 1981. Allan Lamb is run out by Geoff Miller.

INTRODUCTION

All introductions tend to be a mixture of explanations and apologies, and this one is no exception. The apologies must be to those who do not find their own particular favourite 'great' matches among these reports; the explanation is that for the most part I have been guided by those matches that I have seen and remembered.

Inevitably my memory has been refreshed by reference to my own notes, to *Pelham Cricket Year* and, of course, to *Wisden*, the indispensible aid in any cricket research. But I have been helped, too, by the work of the *Limited-Overs Cricket Information Group* and the *Association of Cricket Statisticians*. To one man in particular I owe very great thanks. He is Victor Isaacs, the scorer of Hampshire CCC, and one whose dynamism has made him a friend and ally of all who love the game.

The term 'great' is an over-used one. The leaning to hyperbole in all writing on sport is an ever present danger and when one reflects in tranquillity, the agonies of the moment did not scar one for life as it seemed that they would at the time. I hope, however, that all of the matches reported in this volume have something to commend them, something that lifts them above the ordinary.

There was an initial fear that every match I included would be one in which the result was only decided in the last over until which time all hung in the balance with both sides courting danger. It can be realised that an uninterrupted diet of such matches would, in the end, prove indigestible. There are, of course, several matches of this nature in the collection, but they are balanced by others whose quality lies in the character or performance of an individual or a team.

The limited-over game has its detractors and only a fool would suggest that it can replace the first-class game entirely, but its advent brought finance and renewed vigour to cricket, and we are grateful for both. As John Arlott remarked, the introduction of limited-over cricket has been the most important change in the game in the past fifty years. It has been responsible for better fielding and for some deep thinking. Above all, it has given many people a great deal of pleasure and has drawn to cricket grounds several who had never been before.

ARMY v ROYAL AIR FORCE

At Lord's

14 June 1943

Great one-day cricket matches did not begin with the Gillette Cup in 1963, for one-day matches of sorts have always been part of the game's history.

There is a long tradition of county sides playing local club sides on Sundays, the money received from the sales of score-cards and brochures going to the beneficiary of the year. Such matches have been reduced in number since the advent of the John Player League, but they still take place at the end of the season. Inevitably they are matches of humour and fellowship and rarely produce very serious cricket.

Some of the very greatest of one-day matches were played at Lord's during the war when the receipts were donated to the Red Cross, the Army and Navy Benevolent Fund, or some other appropriate cause. The excitement and enthusiasm generated by those matches played nearly forty years ago, at a time of great stress, still reverberates. Those who saw them will never forget them.

The Whitsun match at Lord's was always a game of particular splendour. The annual contest between Middlesex and Sussex has seen many great occasions. It was in this match, in 1936, that Denis Compton made his debut, and before his time, it was a game in which 'Patsy' Hendren played some of his most memorable innings.

The Whitsun weekend of 1943 was in keeping with the fine tradition and provided some of the most spectacular cricket ever seen at Lord's.

On Whit Saturday, 12 June, the Civil Defence beat the Army by six wickets. Harold Gimblett played a wonderful innings of 124. After two wickets had fallen for 39, he and Jim Parks, senior, added 200 at *two* runs a minute. The target of 253 was reached in under forty (eight-ball) overs. The real glory, however, was saved until the Monday.

Twenty-two thousand people packed into Lord's that bank holiday Monday to see the Army play the RAF. The weather was uncertain. There were four interruptions for rain in the early part of the day and at one time the ground was left covered with a layer of white hailstones which seemed to have ended play for the day, but, in this time of war, there was a willingness to entertain and desire to snatch time out and the match was resumed.

The teams read like a Test trial, but the Army bowling was weakened by the withdrawal of Stan Nichols, the Essex all-rounder.

Wyatt won the toss and asked the Army to bat. Jack Robertson and Charlie Harris batted well on an easy wicket and began with a stand of 66. Then there was a stoppage for rain, and as soon as play resumed, Austin Matthews found the edge of Robertson's bat and Ken James took a fine catch behind the stumps. In the space of the next twenty-two deliveries, Harris, Compton and Bartlett all went the same way while Matthews conceded only four runs. During this spell, too, Sellers was dropped at fine-leg.

At the time none could recall if the first four wickets of an innings had ever before fallen to the same bowler/wicket-keeper combination.

Matthews was an excellent fast medium bowler who played for England against New Zealand in 1937, his one and only Test. Ken James was the first New Zealand Test keeper. In 1933, he came to live in England and qualified for Northants for whom he played from 1935 until the outbreak of war. He was the most elegant of wicket-keepers, anticipating John Murray in his sartorial appearance and fluency of gesture.

The Army's innings was further interrupted by the weather, but by tea the rain had relented and Tom Pearce, who had shared a useful stand with Brian Sellers, declared at 5.15 with the score at 168 for 8. This left the RAF ninety-five minutes in which to make the runs.

In the absence of Nichols, Perks and Garland-Wells opened the attack for the Army. Reg Perks was a quick bowler of character and endeavour. He served Worcestershire splendidly, and, in the last year before the war, played twice for England. His best seasons were lost to the war, for he was thirty-five in

1946 though he still had nine years of opening the Worcestershire bowling in front of him.

Cyril Washbrook and Les Berry gave immediate indication
that the RAF would press for victory. In forty minutes they
scored 55 before Washbrook, who was never able to force the
pace with quite the same ease as Berry, fell to Perks.

Bill Edrich now joined Les Berry in a partnership which
remains quick in the memory for its quality, excitement, richness
of stroke-play and sheer audacity.

Berry was one of the game's great professionals and carried
the Leicestershire batting for twenty years. During that time he
rarely had an opportunity to indulge himself as he did at Lord's
that afternoon. Partnering him was a man who has enjoyed
every minute of his cricketing life and whose greatest glories
still lay ahead.

Against Perks, Garland-Wells, Doug Wright and Leyland, runs
came at ten an over. The crowd was in a state of constant excitement and there was an almost continuous roar of approval.

This was no Sunday league slog of later years. There was no
retreating to square-leg in an attempt to slash the ball through
the off-side field. Here were bowlers endeavouring to get wickets
and batsmen responding with strokes of power and elegance.

Ultimately, Pearce was forced to remove his slip so that all
but Billy Griffith were in front of the wicket. Still those scintil-
lating drives beat the field.

At ten minutes to seven the RAF were victorious. Berry and
Edrich had made the last 114 in forty-four minutes. The weather
of the early day was forgotten. The cricket transcended any discomfort from the skies and it warmed the hearts of those who
were there for many a winter.

There is an epilogue. It may be apocryphal. Bill Edrich
maintains that the night before the match he had taken an RAF
side to the BBC for a 'spelling bee'. As captain he had first
knock. He was asked to spell 'Antirrhinum'. It was not one of
his words. Decline started from that point.

At the end of a depressing contest he turned to his dejected
team and said, 'There's only one thing to do, lads. We'll spend
the rest of the night at the Cabaret Club.'

And they did. Which might explain why he batted so well the
next day.

ARMY *v* ROYAL AIR FORCE
at Lord's
14 June 1943

Army

Capt J.D. Robertson (Middx)	c James, b Matthews	30
Sgt C.B. Harris (Notts)	c James, b Matthews	30
2nd Lt M. Leyland (Yorks)	b Matthews	15
Capt H.T. Bartlett (Sussex)	c James, b Matthews	3
Pte L.H. Compton (Middx)	c James, b Matthews	2
Major A.B. Sellers (Yorks)	c Bedser, b Robinson	35
Capt T.N. Pearce (Essex) (capt)	not out	33
Major H.M. Garland-Wells (Surrey)	c and b Bedser	0
• Major S.C. Griffith (Sussex)	c Matthews, b Todd	6
Lt D.V.P. Wright (Kent)	not out	1
Bombdr R.T.P. Perks (Worcs)		
Extras	b 7, lb 4, w 1, nb 1	13
	(for 8 wkts, dec)	168

	O	M	R	W
Edrich	6	—	40	—
Matthews	17	1	41	5
Todd	10	1	30	1
Bedser	11	2	33	1
Robinson	4	—	11	1

fall of wickets
1—66, 2—67, 3—73, 4—75, 5—108, 6—144, 7—147, 8—158

Royal Air Force

Sgt C. Washbrook (Lancs)	c Bartlett, b Perks	31
Sgt L.G. Berry (Leics)	not out	73
Sqdn Ldr W.J. Edrich (Middx)	not out	53
Extras	lb 1, w 3, nb 8	12
	(for 1 wkt)	169

F/O R.E.S. Wyatt (Warw) (capt), Sqdn Ldr L.E.G. Ames (Kent), Sgt L.J. Todd
(Kent), Sgt G. Cox (Sussex), LAC K.C. James (Northants), Cpl E.P. Robinson
(Yorks), Sgt A.V. Bedser (Surrey) and Flt Lt A.D.G. Matthews (Glam) did not bat

	O	M	R	W
Perks	8	—	40	1
Garland-Wells	5	—	36	—
Wright	5	—	51	—
Leyland	3	—	30	—

fall of wickets
1—55

Royal Air Force won by 9 wickets

SURREY v OLD ENGLAND

At the Oval

23 May 1946

The golden age is always just out of reach. It is the one of which we caught glimpses or heard legends in our youth.

Sir Neville Cardus, the doyen of cricket writers, had his first book published in 1922, and his last after the Second World War, yet the heroes, McLaren, Trumper, Ranjitsinhji, whose achievements and personalities he fixed permanently in our minds with his pen, had ceased to play before that first book was published. Nostalgia is an integral part of cricket.

In 1946, we rejoiced again that the game, at least in shape and structure, was as it had been before man's latest insanity. There were loud complaints that it was not as good as it had been, but then it never is, and mostly this was a time of celebration.

One of the celebrations was at The Oval, where the centenary of the Surrey club and of the use of the ground for cricket had been reached. There was an inspired idea for part of these centenary festivities: Surrey would play Old England in a one-day match.

The term 'Old England' has been used often since, but frequently those who represent the veterans are but barely out of the first-class game and have remained constantly in front of the public on the television screens.

The team that assembled to represent Old England at The Oval on Thursday, 23 May 1946, was separated from those who had worshipped their play by a decade which included a savage war.

Only Brooks, the former Surrey wicket-keeper, of the Old England side had not won a Test cap, and, including the umpires, Hobbs and Strudwick, there were 370 Test caps present for Old England that Thursday, and these had been won in the days when five Tests a season was a maximum and when series against India, New Zealand and West Indies merited only three Tests.

Fifteen thousand people flocked to The Oval to celebrate the occasion and to welcome the heroes of the past, and to see both teams introduced to King George VI. The band of the East Surrey Regiment played during the day and the gods of cricket smiled upon the event with the most glorious day of the summer. The cricket graced the occasion.

Maurice Tate opened the attack with all his old accuracy, and if he lacked something of his former 'nip', he still set an example in line and length. Then came 'Tich' Freeman, arm a little lower, googly not used, but with the leg-break and top-spinner fizzing off a perfect length as they had done for Kent for nearly twenty years. It was ten years since he had been seen on a first-class cricket field, but here he was, at the age of fifty-eight, still able to test batsmen of quality with the subtle variations of his bowling. He deceived Fishlock and Fender took a fine catch.

Gregory and Squires put on 111 for the second wicket and then Percy Fender, at last captain of an England side, an honour which many felt should have come to him twenty years earlier, dismissed Gregory and Barling with successive deliveries to cause great excitement.

There were no more traumas in the Surrey innings, however, and Bennett declared at 248 for 6, leaving Old England nearly three and a quarter hours in which to get the runs.

Their innings began most depressingly. The immaculate Sutcliffe and the old Oval favourite, Andy Sandham, were both out to Eddie Watts with only two runs scored. There was a stir of embarrassment among the crowd. There was a sense of unease that this match could have been a great mistake, for men of nearly sixty, however fit, cannot compete with first-class cricketers who are in constant practice.

Woolley was joined by Hendren. And the clock was turned back twenty-five years.

The most elegant left-hander in the history of the game, a man who, with a bat in his hand, was a vision of beauty, drove and glanced with the ease that had delighted crowds before the First World War. The fifty-nine years slipped away and we remembered again those afternoons in Kent, 'full of the air and peaceful sunshine of England'.

At the other end was the perkiest character that cricket had ever known, forcing gleefully with all his old gusto. He teased and delighted, and always there was that slight suggestion of irreverence that made him irresistible.

They added 102 before Woolley fell to Alec Bedser, who was to play his first Test match a month later. Hendren and Jardine now had the audacity to press for victory in a stand of 108.

Douglas Jardine, defiantly sporting his Oxford Harlequin cap, was cheered from the wicket, a tribute to his polished technique, academic skill and grace, and a belated thanks for services rendered. How trite the fury of body-line seemed after the carnage of war.

Shortly before the close Hendren drove at Alec Bedser and lofted a catch to Barling. At fifty-seven years of age, he had batted two and three quarter hours and hit eight fours in his innings of 94. Mingled with the joy and the waves of applause was a tinge of sadness that he had not managed the other six runs, but what pleasure he had given.

Old England failed by seventeen runs to snatch victory, but, in the circumstances, a draw was a most fitting result.

The day was completed with a dance in the long room of the pavilion and a couple of days later Percy Fender wrote to *The Times* to express the thanks of his team.

'More than once while we were fielding,' he wrote, 'a thought came to my mind that the warmth of the welcome, the size and the enthusiasm of the great crowd, and, above all, the presence of His Majesty, seemed to convey a message to all the younger generation of cricketers, not only in this country, but all over the world. A message telling them that where cricket is concerned, public memory, in spite of the old adage, is not short: a message to inspire all young cricketers, and to urge them to achievements in the game greater than their wildest dreams conjured up.

'Such a welcome as was given to "Old England", collectively and individually, must surely be a public assurance that those who can carve for themselves a little niche in the greatest of games can always be sure of a warm place in the heart of all lovers of cricket.'

Surrey *v* Old England was a game that was not great in the sense of dramatic climax and thrilling finish, but it did have a greatness uniquely its own.

SURREY *v* OLD ENGLAND
At The Oval
23 May 1946

Surrey

R.J. Gregory	b Fender	62
L.B. Fishlock	c Fender, b Freeman	25
H.S. Squires	b Holmes	68
T.H. Barling	lbw, b Fender	0
J.F. Parker	c and b Allom	12
A.J. McIntyre	not out	39
E.A. Bedser	c Brooks, b Allom	23
E.A. Watts	not out	13
N.H. Bennett (capt)		
G.J. Whittaker		
* G.S. Mobey		
A.V. Bedser		
Extras	b 5, lb 1	6
	(for 6 wkts, dec)	248

	O	M	R	W
Tate	8	1	26	—
Allom	17	2	76	2
Freeman	15	3	58	1
Holmes	8	1	36	1
Fender	8	—	46	2

Old England

H. Sutcliffe	lbw, b Watts	1
A. Sandham	c A.V. Bedser, b Watts	1
F.E. Woolley	c McIntyre, b A.V. Bedser	62
E.P. Hendren	c Barling, b A.V. Bedser	94
D.R. Jardine	b Parker	54
P.G.H. Fender (capt)	not out	12
D.J. Knight	not out	2
M.W. Tate		
E.R.T. Holmes		
M.J.C. Allom		
* E.W.J. Brooks		
A.P. Freeman		
Extras	b 3, lb 2, nb 1	6
	(for 5 wkts)	232

	O	M	R	W
A.V. Bedser	21	3	45	2
Watts	18	3	83	2
Parker	15	—	51	1
Squires	7	—	29	—
E.A. Bedser	4	2	3	—
McIntyre	2	—	11	—
Gregory	1	—	4	—

Match Drawn

SUSSEX v WORCESTERSHIRE

GILLETTE CUP FINAL

At Lord's

7 September 1963

By the mid-fifties there was great concern at the vast drop in the number of people watching first-class cricket. One and a half million spectators were lost in the nineteen-fifties, a decline so serious as to cause the MCC to set up a special committee under the chairmanship of Harry Altham to investigate the state of the game and suggest remedies.

It was Altham's committee which first proposed a knock-out competition. It is difficult for us to realise now that the suggestion was not greeted with enthusiasm and that it was only the continuing deterioration of cricket's finances that finally prompted the instigation of the knock-out competition.

Although the sole purpose of the knock-out competition was to supplement county finances, there was concern that in the event of bad weather it might well prove to have the reverse effect and be a drain on county funds. It was this concern that brought about the approach to the Gillette Company who agreed to underwrite the competition. So 'The First-Class Counties Knock-Out Competition for the Gillette Cup' was born, a sixty-five over competition quickly to be reduced to sixty overs because of the number of twilight finishes in its first year and just as quickly to become known simply as 'The Gillette Cup'.

The new competition had an inauspicious beginning. The first Gillette Cup match was between Lancashire and Leicestershire at Old Trafford. The weather was wet and miserable and the game took two days to complete. There were only a few spectators who were willing to brave the elements. Lancashire won easily and Peter Marner, who scored 121, was made Man-of-the-Match by Frank Woolley. Maurice Hallam also hit a hundred in this game and there was continuing hostility to the idea of selecting a Man-of-the-Match.

There was much to learn in the early days. Before a ball was bowled in the competition most captains had decided that such a contest was no place for a spin bowler. The first final was to show them the error of this thinking. The early matches revealed that whilst thought had been given to the choice of bowlers none had been given to the fields that should be employed.

Sussex travelled to Tunbridge Wells to meet Kent in the first round. There was a large and happy crowd on this beautiful ground. Ted Dexter won the toss and Sussex batted first. Colin Cowdrey set a conventional field. Sussex lost both openers with only 27 scored, but then Dexter and Suttle came together in a good stand. As the ball was hit around the Neville ground Cowdrey made no compromise in his field placings, continuing to attack with slips and gully and other close catching positions. Sussex reached 314 for 7 in their sixty-five overs. Young Derek Underwood conceded 87 runs in the eleven overs he bowled. The limit at that time was fifteen overs per bowler.

When Kent batted, they too made a bad start losing Luckhurst and Leary for 19 before Peter Richardson and Colin Cowdrey looked as if they could bring Kent close to victory. Ted Dexter explains his tactics:

'There was only one man who looked like doing any good and that was Peter Richardson. It was not my main intention to get him out. I just set the field back, allowed him to take a single, then bowled tight to the other batsman to force him to make the runs and not Richardson. There were boos and screams and everyone thought this was a rotten thing to do — there was so much sympathy for Richardson that he received the team award — but there it was, I had shown people what they could be let in for.'

Dexter's field placing had taught people a salutory lesson, but it was a lesson that took a long time to digest. The following season Clayton, the Lancashire wicket-keeper, demonstrated his contempt for the far flung field set by Warwickshire in the semi-final by showing little inclination to attempt to score runs. The game ended in a Warwickshire victory amid boos, a slow hand-clap and cat-calls. Clayton and Lancashire parted company at the end of the season.

What was becoming readily apparent was that the limited-over game was not simply a merry slog, but a game which demanded

much thought and a reconsideration of traditional tactics. It
was also apparent that, in Ted Dexter, Sussex had a cricketer
and captain ideally suited for the game.

His qualities as a cricketer were easily recognisable. He was
an attractive, hard-hitting, fast-scoring batsman; a fine field; and
a medium pace bowler of accuracy and intelligence. What was
not so well known was that he was a deep thinker on the game
who responded to challenge with the calculating brain of a
grand master. At first he was not attracted to the limited-over
game, but he saw that Sussex possessed the talent to succeed in
this type of cricket, and he accepted the Gillette Cup competition as a new and intriguing problem which he had to solve.

He studied the bowlers at his disposal and determined that
success would come from the use of seam bowling, accurate
rather than attacking, backed by a carefully placed defensive
field. The essence of the bowling was to be relentless efficiency.
The batting had to be brisk so that the number of runs obtained
would put extra pressure on the opponents. It all sounds naive
and simple now, but it was Sussex alone who first employed the
formula. Others followed, but Sussex had won the Gillette Cup
twice before anyone could exploit equal talents to such purpose.

Following the defeat of Kent, Sussex met Yorkshire at Hove.
They won a thrilling match by 22 runs. Parks and Dexter were
the heroes, but the most important fact was that the attendance
for the match equalled the ground record. The misgivings that
authority may have had about the knock-out competition were
being dispelled by the enthusiasm of the fans who were flocking
through the turnstiles to see the matches and bringing economic
salvation to first-class cricket.

In the semi-finals Sussex had an easy victory over Northants
at Northampton, with Dexter hitting 115 and Parks 71, and
Worcestershire crushed Lancashire at Worcester. Flavell took 6
for 14 as Lancashire were bowled out for 59, and Worcestershire got the runs in sixty-one balls for the loss of one wicket.

It is hard to imagine that the weather could have been more
unkind than it was for the first of the great one-day finals at
Lord's. It was cold and cloudy all day, and there were periods
of drizzle. The match ended in light rain and semi-darkness, but
twenty-five thousand people stayed to the very end to witness
an enthralling game.

Dexter was true to his theories. He omitted the left-arm spinner Ronnie Bell, and relied on a pace attack of Bates, Buss, Thomson, Snow and himself. In spite of the damp conditions, he decided to bat when he won the toss, again keeping to his tried formula.

It was soon obvious that run-scoring would not be easy on the wet wicket and saturated outfield. Langridge and Oakman gave the side a very solid start, but they found no opportunity to increase the scoring rate once they had settled. They survived the opening pace attack of Flavell and Carter, but were soon in trouble when Kenyon turned to his spinners.

The off-spin of Horton and the slow left arm of Gifford and Slade were devastating on the damp pitch and the batsmen floundered. Gifford took four of the first five wickets to fall, and Sussex, 62 before a wicket fell, lost six wickets in doubling the score. The big guns of Dexter and Suttle were silenced, and it was left to Jim Parks to give the Sussex innings any substance.

There are many who regret that Jim Parks was ever persuaded to take up wicket-keeping. He kept for England in over forty Tests, but he was never in the top flight and the imperfections of his wicket-keeping detracted from the undoubted brilliance of his batting. He was an exciting player, quick and graceful in movement, ever looking for the scoring shot, particularly ruthless on spinners.

Curbing some of his natural aggression on the uncertain wicket, he alone played Gifford and Slade with confidence, hitting a six and four fours in his ninety-minute innings. When he fell to Slade, Sussex had little more to offer and they failed to last their full quota of overs.

Norman Gifford finished with 4 for 33 and a spinner was to receive the first Man-of-the-Match award in a Gillette Cup final. It was an ironic answer to those who said that the spinner had no place in this type of cricket.

Gifford's success was an irony upon which Ted Dexter could muse. His own left-arm spinner was in the pavilion and, on a spinner's wicket, he had an all seam attack.

There was an early, and important, success for Sussex, however, when the redoubtable Don Kenyon was lbw to Tony Buss with the score on 7. As first Horton, and then Headley and Graveney moved the score along steadily, it became obvious that the Sussex seam attack could not exploit this early success. Needing to score at only just over two and a half runs an over, Worcestershire could counter Dexter's tactics easily in these conditions. In Dexter's own words, 'My classic formula had encountered the worst possible conditions for its application.' The medium-pacers were neither containing the Worcestershire batsmen, nor getting them out.

Quick to reappraise a situation, Dexter turned to an unexpected source, Alan Oakman, who had never bowled his off-breaks in limited-over cricket, and Ken Suttle, who had sent down five overs of his left-arm slows against Yorkshire without success. He told them that it was a spinner's wicket and that they were the only two who could win the match for Sussex.

Concentrating on keeping an impeccable length, Oakman caused uncertainty among the batsmen with his exceptionally high delivery. Suttle, too, concentrated on accuracy.

The flow of runs dried up. Astute field placing and Oakman's control meant that the off-spinner yielded only 17 runs in thirteen overs. Most important, he induced Tom Graveney to give Dexter a stinging catch. The pressure was now on Worcestershire.

The light deteriorated and Dexter brought back his quicker bowlers. John Snow bowled Gifford and Flavell in one over and Worcestershire were 133 for 9 and seemingly well beaten. Roy Booth was still there and he was joined by Bob Carter.

Carter defended stubbornly and Booth lashed out. The gap between the two sides narrowed. Dexter was calming his forces and rearranging his field, but Booth's powerful hitting had forced him to place nine men around the boundary. With eleven balls to go, Worcestershire needed 15 runs for victory, but then Booth and Carter were forced to attempt one quick run too many and Bob Carter was run out.

The last wicket stand had produced 21 runs. They had been scored in the gloom and light drizzle to the accompaniment of a constant roar of appreciative excitement. As Dexter held the cup aloft no doubts remained in any quarter as to the wisdom and efficacy of the new knock-out competition.

Peter Wilson, that most respected of sports writers, set the seal of approval in his forthright style:

'If there has ever been a triumphant sporting experiment, the knock-out cricket cup for the Gillette Trophy was that experiment. A year ago, anyone suggesting that on a cold, damp September Saturday afternoon, Lord's, the temple of tradition, could be transformed into a reasonable replica of Wembley on its Cup Final day, would have been sent post haste to the nearest psychiatrist's couch. Yet that's what happened — a sell-out with rosettes, singing, cheers, jeers and counter-cheers. Plus a hark-a-way on a Worcestershire hunting horn when England and Sussex captain, Ted Dexter, was dismissed by a fine diving slip catch by Broadbent. This may not have been cricket to the purists, but by golly it was just the stuff the doctor ordered. And I am sure Dr W.G. Grace would have been one of the doctors concurring. It's sufficient to say that the Gillette Cup may well in future years assume the status of such established "Cups" as even the FA, the Rugby League or, stretching the imagination, the Davis or the Canada Cup.'

SUSSEX *v* WORCESTERSHIRE
Gillette Cup Final
at Lord's
7 September 1963

Sussex

R.J. Langridge	b Gifford	34
A.S.M Oakman	c Slade, b Gifford	19
K.G. Suttle	b Gifford	9
E.R. Dexter (capt)	c Broadbent, b Horton	3
* J.M. Parks	b Slade	57
L.J. Lenham	c Booth, b Gifford	7
G.C. Cooper	lbw, b Slade	0
N.I. Thomson	lbw, b Flavell	1
A. Buss	c Booth, b Carter	3
J.A. Snow	b Flavell	10
D.L. Bates	not out	3
Extras	b 9, lb 10, nb 3	22
		168

	O	M	R	W
Flavell	14.2	3	31	2
Carter	12	1	39	1
Slade	11	2	23	2
Gifford	15	4	33	4
Horton	8	1	20	1

fall of wickets
1—62, 2—67, 3—76, 4—98, 5—118, 6—123, 7—134, 8—142, 9—157

Worcestershire

D. Kenyon (capt)	lbw, b Buss	1
M.J. Horton	c and b Buss	26
R.G.A. Headley	c Snow, b Bates	25
T.W. Graveney	c Dexter, b Oakman	29
D.W. Richardson	c Parks, b Thomson	3
R.G. Broadbent	c Bates, b Snow	13
* R. Booth	not out	33
D.N.F. Slade	b Buss	3
N. Gifford	b Snow	0
J.A. Flavell	b Snow	0
R.G. Carter	run out	2
Extras	b 8, lb 9, nb 2	19
		154

	O	M	R	W
Thomson	13.2	4	35	1
Buss	15	2	39	3
Oakman	13	4	17	1
Suttle	5	2	11	—
Bates	9	2	20	1
Snow	8	—	13	3

fall of wickets
1−7, 2−38, 3−80, 4−91, 5−103, 6−128, 7−132, 8−133, 9−133

Sussex won by 14 runs

YORKSHIRE v SURREY

GILLETTE CUP FINAL

At Lord's

4 September 1965

Victory at the last possible moment, achieved at the greatest possible risk, expunges all that has gone before so that through its dramatic climax alone a match may remain in the memory and be deemed 'great'.

There are occasions when greatness is achieved early in the day, when bowling in the opening overs is so destructive, or when an innings is played which is of such magnitude that all that follows is irrelevant. Such was the case in the Gillette Cup final of 1965 when Yorkshire became the only side to score three hundred runs in the final and when they recorded the biggest win in any of the eighteen finals of that splendid competition. They beat Surrey by 175 runs.

1965 was the third year of Brian Close's captaincy of the county. It was the year that Freddie Trueman played his sixty-seventh and final Test, and it was the year that Geoff Boycott began to establish himself in the England side.

He had made his Test debut the year before and had scored his first Test century, at The Oval.

By 1965, he had been a Yorkshire player for three years. He had quickly formed the reputation of being a solid, reliable opener with an unwillingness to play shots or to take risks. In two years time he would be dropped from the Test side after scoring 246 not out against India. The innings lasted nine and a half hours and his omission from the England side was a disciplinary action against his slow scoring which was seen as not in the best interests of the side. His self-imposed three-year exile from Test cricket was still nearly a decade away.

What mixed emotions the man has aroused in his long, distinguished and controversial career. As Christopher Martin-Jenkins has astutely observed, Boycott is 'A profoundly sensitive man for whom outstanding success and world-wide fame have created intense personal problems.'

His utter dedication to the perfection of his own batting technique, the eradication of all error, has not always won him the approval of his fellow professionals who have interpreted his approach as being selfish and contrary to the demands of the team as a whole. Authority, at county and national level, has often held a similar view regarding Boycott's relentless application. He has had many trials with which he has had to contend, the loss of the Yorkshire captaincy and the failure of his bid to become captain of England, his greatest ambition, being the most severe.

Boycott's occasional isolation, when seemingly he has stood alone against cricket's government, has always been compensated for by a loyal following of supporters who have seen him as a folk-hero, a working-class champion vying with the powers of reaction. This miscasting has increased the enigma surrounding the man.

But we digress. This was the third Gillette Cup final. The first two had been won by Sussex, who had been well beaten by Middlesex in the quarter-finals. Yorkshire had had no easy task in reaching the final and their semi-final at Edgbaston had been so mutilated by the weather as to take three days to complete, Warwickshire finally being beaten by twenty runs.

The other semi-final had seen Surrey gain a marvellous victory over Middlesex after being set to make 251. This was a good Surrey side. Mickey Stewart, as always, led by example and there were Edrich and Barrington to give further solidity to the batting. In bowling there was the exuberant, promising youth of Geoff Arnold backed by two fine county bowlers in Sydenham and Gibson.

Inspired by his county's success in chasing a large total against Middlesex, Stewart asked Yorkshire to bat when he won the toss; it was a decision which he was to regret and for which he was to be severely criticised.

There was much to support Stewart's decision. Torrential rain throughout Friday and in the early hours of Saturday morning had left Lord's awash. The ground staff worked feverishly to clear the lakes from the outfield. They borrowed drying machines from The Oval and their splendid efforts were rewarded when play was able to start at twelve o'clock.

The conditions were still very soggy and the dampness of the outfield suggested that this would be a low scoring game.

Taylor was caught at slip by Barrington off Sydenham with the score at 22. It was really the last success that Surrey had all day.

Let us concern ourselves with the facts of what followed. Having begun slowly, Boycott and Close gradually increased the tempo as they added 192 for the second wicket. Close hit one six and seven fours in his innings of 79. Trueman was sent in at number four to swing the bat, which he did to good effect. John Hampshire and Don Wilson also hit lustily, but there remains only one shining memory from the Yorkshire innings — Geoff Boycott.

His score was 146. He hit three sixes and fifteen fours. It remained the highest innings ever played in a Gillette final, and the best. He had not had a good season for Yorkshire. His highest score in first-class cricket in 1965 was 95, but that September afternoon at Lord's all was right. At this distance it is hard to convey quite the greatness of that innings.

There are innings which by their influence on the course of the match fix themselves in time. There are others, like the one played by David Hughes of Lancashire and mentioned later in this volume, which have a violence and a brevity which demand attention. Rarely are there innings of perfection, but the innings that Boycott played against Surrey at Lord's in 1965 reached heights which most never attain.

It was without blemish. Not only did the man not give a chance, but he did not violate the art of batsmanship. He is above crudity and the acquisition of technique has been too hard won a prize for it to be prostituted for quick runs. One cannot point to that innings and say 'Ah, he hooked wonderfully' or 'He drove magnificently', for that would be to suggest that he accomplished these shots better than others and this was not so. The beauty lay in the fact that here was the artist who was the complete master. The colours were mixed right and no part of the picture dulled in comparison to another. Every detail was there as in the vibrant brushwork of a Canaletto. There was no bludgeoning to success. Every ball was met with the correct shot, firm to defend, quick to attack, and all in perfect symmetry.

When he was out the game was over. Surrey faced an impossible task. They began bravely enough but Trueman then dismissed Edrich, Smith and Barrington within the space of four

deliveries. Stewart battled on, but after he had been stumped
Tindall played a courageous lone hand. He watched Illingworth
take the wickets of Storey, Edwards and Gibson in one over and
he himself fell victim to Close so that Surrey were all out in the
forty-first over, suffering the heaviest defeat in any of the
Gillette finals.

Doug Insole made Geoff Boycott Man-of-the Match. No one
was surprised. Since that day Boycott has scored many thousands
of runs. He hit his hundredth hundred in a Test match. He has
become the scorer of more runs in Test cricket than any other
player. He has averaged more than a hundred in a season. His
desire to occupy the crease has grown with the years. He has
eliminated any shot that could cause him to lose his wicket; the
hook, for example, he no longer plays. His concentration on
longevity has meant that he has, on occasions, been omitted
from the Yorkshire side in one-day matches and that England,
too, have had doubts about his suitability for the limited-over
game. In Adelaide, shortly before Christmas 1978, he batted
number eleven for the England touring side because they were
going for quick runs in an attempt to beat South Australia.

Yet there are twenty-five thousand people who were at
Lord's on 4 September 1965, and many more who watched on
television who believe that Boycott played that day the greatest
innings ever played in a limited-over match. Some of us believe,
too, that it was the finest innings of Boycott's illustrious career.

YORKSHIRE *v* SURREY
Gillette Cup Final
at Lord's
4 September 1965

Yorkshire

G. Boycott	C Storey, b Barrington	146
K. Taylor	c Barrington, b Sydenham	9
D.B. Close (capt)	c Edrich, b Gibson	79
F.S. Trueman	b Arnold	24
J.H. Hampshire	not out	38
D. Wilson	not out	11
D.E.V. Padgett		
P.J. Sharpe		
R. Illingworth		
R.A. Hutton		
* J.G. Binks		
Extras	b 3, lb 4, nb 3	10
	(for 4 wickets)	317

	O	M	R	W
Arnold	13	3	51	1
Sydenham	13	1	67	1
Gibson	13	1	66	1
Storey	13	2	33	—
Tindall	3	—	36	—
Barrington	5	—	54	1

fall of wickets
1—22, 2—214, 3—248, 4—292

Surrey

M.J. Stewart (capt)	st Binks, b Wilson	33
J.H. Edrich	c Illingworth, b Trueman	15
W.A. Smith	lbw, b Trueman	0
K.F. Barrington	c Binks, b Trueman	0
R.A.E. Tindall	c Wilson, b Close	57
S.J. Storey	lbw, b Illingworth	1
M.J. Edwards	b Illingworth	0
D. Gibson	lbw, b Illingworth	0
* A. Long	b Illingworth	17
G. Arnold	not out	3
D.A.D. Sydenham	b Illingworth	8
Extras	b 4, lb 4	8
		142

	O	M	R	W
Trueman	9	—	31	3
Hutton	8	3	17	—
Wilson	9	—	45	1
Illingworth	11.4	1	29	5
Close	3	—	12	1

fall of wickets
1—27, 2—27, 3—27, 4—75, 5—76, 6—76, 7—76, 8—130, 9—132

Yorkshire won by 175 runs

LANCASHIRE v GLOUCESTERSHIRE

GILLETTE CUP SEMI-FINAL

At Old Trafford

28 July 1971

Events establish themselves through clearly defined images. The funeral of Sir Winston Churchill, for example, is fixed for many by the solitary image of Clement Attlee, old and tired, sitting on the steps of St Paul's Cathedral in isolated introspection. From the novel, *Tess of the D'Urbevilles*, there comes across the years the one clear picture of a young girl awaking in a field at dawn to find herself surrounded by dead and dying birds.

. Cricket is no exception. Hammond is seen always in the moment of the cover drive. Compton is crystalised in the sweep. Randall does perpetual cartwheels to celebrate the return of the Ashes.

And Manchester, 28 July 1971? Twenty-three thousand people watching cricket of the greatest tension. Lights shining brightly from the pavilion through the evening gloom. Trains twinkling in the adjacent station. Dusk illuminated by the brilliance of the cricket.

These are images from 8.50 pm in a game which had begun nearly ten hours earlier. Lancashire versus Gloucestershire, Gillette Cup semi-final.

For Lancashire these were the great days of the limited-over game. So many people crowded into Old Trafford on a Sunday that Jack Bond remarked later that he came to hate Mondays.

'Who was he, this Jack Bond?' one hears asked. He did not place his name in the record books as a prolific run-getter, nor did he bowl, and yet under him Lancashire were transformed from a disjointed rabble into one of the most efficient one-day sides that cricket has seen.

His effect upon the side made him worth twice as much as many cricketers with more impressive batting averages and achievements at international level.

There are men in the history of cricket whose achievement

can only be measured in terms of the electrifying contribution
that they have made to sides through sheer force of personality
and qualities of leadership. Stuart Surridge was of this number,
so were Jack Cheetham of South Africa, Brian Taylor of Essex,
J.R. Burnet and A.B. Sellers of Yorkshire, and Wilf Wooller of
Glamorgan; and so was Jack Bond of Lancashire.

In this game, as in so many others, Bond's contribution was
to be one of phlegmatic inspiration, the inculcation of the belief
that victory was possible when defeat seemed inevitable.

The first honours of this day, however, went to Tony Brown,
the Gloucestershire captain, who won the toss and had no
hesitation in deciding to bat first on a good wicket.

David Green, returning to play against his old county, opened
the Gloucestershire innings with the reliable Ron Nicholls. The
Lancashire attack which confronted them was led by Peter
Lever and Ken Shuttleworth, both of whom had become England
bowlers the previous winter, in Australia. Neither Green nor
Nicholls was troubled by reputation and Gloucestershire were
given the soundest of starts. The score had reached 57 before
Green was run out.

Nicholls now played quite splendidly. Throughout his career
he remained essentially a local cricketer. It was never suggested
that he should play for England, but few men ever served a
county better or seemed so much part of its soil. He was not a
great stylist, but he moved with quick determination as befitted
a professional goalkeeper. He reached an admirable 53 out of 87
before he was deceived by a ball of low trajectory from Jack
Simmons and was bowled.

There had been a delay in play of an hour at lunch through
rain, but the wicket remained unaffected. Procter now strode
onto the stage in his customary role of Colossus.

Those mighty shoulders opened in full power as he hit a six
and nine fours. None felt his strength more than the left-arm
spinner David Hughes.

In full cry Procter was a wonderful sight; exciting because
the very nature of his play suggested human vulnerability allied
to the power and invincibility of the gods.

It was Peter Lever who ended the Gloucestershire revels when,
on returning to the attack, he had Procter brilliantly caught
behind by the debonair Engineer.

It was not to Lever, however, but to Jack Simmons that the bowling honours belonged. He has never been either a great spinner or flighter of the ball, but his relentlessly accurate length and his persistent attack on the leg-stump kept within bounds a Gloucestershire innings which had threatened to erupt beyond reach of Lancashire. As it was, 229 seemed a total within the home county's reach, and certainly not a task beyond their capabilities.

David Lloyd and Barry Wood gave them a solid, but slow, start. The first 50 runs took seventeen overs, and Lloyd fell to Tony Brown at 61. Wood and Harry Pilling confirmed this beginning with a stand of good sense, sound application and an increase in tempo. They took the score to 105 and victory had a firm foundation, but Wood was run out and Pilling bowled by Brown.

Gloucestershire now found a hero in John Mortimore and the game turned sharply in their favour. Ever attacking, Mortimore tossed the ball in the air invitingly and spun it appreciably. Clive Lloyd was deceived in the flight and bowled. Farouk Engineer was beaten off the pitch, caught in two minds and hit his wicket. The left-arm medium of Davey accounted for Sullivan and Lancashire had crumpled to 163 for 6.

Now came Bond. In the most crucial stage of the match survival was vital. He and Simmons did more than that. They restored sanity and pressed for victory. The time was 7.30 pm and the light was worsening minute by minute. Undismayed they added 40 in seven overs before Simmons became another Mortimore victim.

Twenty-seven were now required and six overs of the innings remained. It was very dark and Bond could have called a halt at any moment, hoping that the following morning, in more favourable light, he and Hughes could get the necessary runs. Against this reasoning was the fact that Procter and Davey were entitled to bowl four of the last six overs. Gloucestershire had already been on the field for well over three hours and to halt the game now would give the two quicker bowlers the opportunity for a night's rest and recuperation.

There was another consideration, too. This match, which had begun at eleven o'clock, had held the capacity crowd enthralled throughout the day. It was now reaching its dramatic climax and the growing tension could be acutely sensed through the growing dark. To leave the field now would be like bringing the curtain down as Birnam Wood moved to Dunsinane.

Bond's new partner was David Hughes. Hughes was twenty-four years old and had gained his county cap the previous year. He was considered a slow left-arm bowler of promise and a useful batsman whose highest score in a limited-over game was 38 against Notts in the John Player League two years earlier. His career average in first-class cricket was just over 13. He was to wait another ten years before scoring his first hundred in the County Championship.

He had spent his time while Simmons and Bond were engaged in their seventh wicket partnership, sitting in a dark corner of the dressing room to try and accustom his eyes to the 'light'. When he came to the middle Bond suggested to him that they should look for the singles. Hughes nodded agreement, but is quoted as saying, 'If I can see them, skipper, I think I can hit them.'

These nearly proved to be his last words for Mortimore beat and all but bowled him first ball.

The fifty-fifth over was bowled by Davey. It was a fine over and by the end of it Lancashire still needed 25 to win and there remained but five overs in which to get them.

Hughes (2 not out) faced the fifty-sixth over which was to be bowled by John Mortimore who had taken 3 for 57 in ten overs.

Still Mortimore tossed the ball into the air. He was an attacking bowler and a good and brave one and he knew no other way. Quick on his feet, Hughes moved down the wicket and hit the first ball over extra cover for four. He smote lustily at the second delivery. It was a clean, true hit and soared over long-on for a massive six. The crowd became wild and everyone was on his feet. The third ball was slashed through the off-side field and the batsmen scampered two runs. The fourth ball was hit wide of mid-on and they raced through for two more runs.

The fifth ball of the over produced a cover drive of such effortless power and precision that the fielders could only stand in stunned admiration as it raced to the boundary. And then the last ball of the over was swung high over mid-on for six and the scores were level. Twenty-four runs had been scored in the over and in less than four minutes a barely known Lancashire all-rounder, not fully sure of his first team place, had become a national figure whose feat was shown on television to the exclusion of scheduled programmes.

Procter bowled the fifty-seventh over which was to be the last of the innings. All that was needed now was calm. Bond was the perfect casting for this situation. Four balls passed without event, except that the crowd was on the point of invading the pitch every ball. The fifth ball Bond nudged wide of gully and the crowd submerged the ball as the players raced from the pitch as Bond and Hughes went through for the single. It was a memorable victory.

On the strength of that one unforgettable over David Hughes was named Man-of-the-Match. Earlier his eleven overs had cost 68 runs, but in that one inspired over he had faced from John Mortimore he had won the match and stamped his name indelibly on cricket history. His hitting did much to help Lancashire win the final.

It is worth recalling some of the ironies of that day at Old Trafford. Earlier in the season, in a John Player League match at Bristol, Mortimore had taken 3 for 9 in six overs against Lancashire. Four times in the next six years, Gloucestershire were to be thwarted by Lancashire in the Gillette Cup, but, avoiding them in 1973, they reached the final where they beat Sussex in a fine match. It was some consolation for John Mortimore who, like Malcolm Nash, will probably be best remembered for one over in the thousands he bowled in his career when, through no fault of his own, he became the victim of an inspired piece of batting.

LANCASHIRE *v* GLOUCESTERSHIRE
Gillette Cup Semi-Final
at Old Trafford
28 July 1971

Gloucestershire

R.B. Nicholls	b Simmons	53
D.M. Green	run out	21
R.D.V. Knight	c Simmons, b Hughes	31
M.J. Procter	c Engineer, b Lever	65
D.R. Shepherd	lbw, b Simmons	6
M. Bissex	not out	29
A.S. Brown (capt)	c Engineer, b Sullivan	6
H. Jarman	not out	0
J.B. Mortimore		
* B.J. Meyer		
J. Davey		
Extras	b 2, lb 14, w 1, nb 1	18
	(for 6 wkts)	229

	O	M	R	W
Lever	12	3	40	1
Shuttleworth	12	3	33	—
Wood	12	3	39	—
Hughes	11	—	68	1
Simmons	12	3	25	2
Sullivan	1	—	6	1

fall of wickets
1—57, 2—87, 3—113, 4—150, 5—201, 6—210

Lancashire

D. Lloyd	lbw, b Brown	31
B. Wood	run out	50
H. Pilling	b Brown	21
C.H. Lloyd	b Mortimore	34
J. Sullivan	b Davey	10
* F.M. Engineer	hit wkt, b Mortimore	2
J.D. Bond (capt)	not out	16
J. Simmons	b Mortimore	25
D.P. Hughes	not out	26
P. Lever		
K. Shuttleworth		
Extras	b 1, lb 13, nb 1	15
	(for 7 wkts)	230

	O	M	R	W
Procter	10.5	3	38	—
Davey	11	1	22	1
Knight	12	2	42	—
Mortimore	11	—	81	3
Brown	12	—	32	2

fall of wickets
1—61, 2—105, 3—136, 4—156, 5—160, 6—163, 7—203/*Lancashire won by 3 wickets*

YORKSHIRE v DURHAM

GILLETTE CUP, ROUND ONE

At Harrogate

30 June 1973

Between 1959 and 1968, Yorkshire won the County Championship seven times. They also won the Gillette Cup in 1965, as we have noted, and in 1969. In over a decade since then they have failed to win any of the major competitions. In the nineteen-seventies they won only four Gillette Cup matches and for four years, 1970–73, they were beaten in their first match. Yet still the aura of glory hung about them. Faded though their triumphs were, Yorkshire were the side that other sides most wanted to beat and the side that many still considered the hardest to beat.

In 1973, they were drawn at home to Durham in the first round of the Gillette Cup. The first minor county representation in the competition was in 1964, but no minor county had yet been successful against their first-class opponents.

Harrogate was the ground chosen for Yorkshire's encounter with Durham. It was a fitting choice for a festive occasion. In these beautiful surroundings, set among some of the most lovely country in England, Yorkshire batsmen would be able to score a host of runs to entertain their avid followers and their bowlers would account for the minnows with ease.

Geoff Boycott, in his third year as Yorkshire skipper, won the toss and so every advantage seemed to be with the great county. He decided to bat and he and Lumb opened the Yorkshire innings.

The opening bowlers for Durham were John Wilkinson and Alan Old, the rugby international and elder brother of the Yorkshire and England fast bowler. They bowled accurately and with fervour. The first nine overs produced only 18 runs, but such a cautious opening was not unusual in a sixty-over game.

It was a placid start, but nothing seemed amiss, and then Wilkinson bowled Boycott. Boycott was then the leading English batsman. He was the Yorkshire captain and the most difficult batsman in the world to dismiss. To bowl him seemed a near impossibility, but that is what the thirty-one-year-old Wilkinson did. This act in itself was a momentous one, but its effect upon the rest of the Durham side was amazing. Suddenly they were like a team possessed. Their bowling was forked with fire; their fielding touched unsuspected heights.

Ball after ball was sent down on an impeccable length and the Yorkshire innings disintegrated. Sharpe was caught behind off Inglis and Lumb became Lander's first victim.

Brian Lander was a thirty-one-year-old, right-arm, medium pace bowler from Bishop Auckland. He played for the Durham City club and he was captain of the county. In 1977 he was to take 6 for 60 against Staffordshire, but he never bowled better than he did against Yorkshire at Harrogate in June, 1973. He never quite completed his quota of twelve overs for Yorkshire were all out before his twelfth over was finished, by which time he had taken the wickets of Hampshire, Richard Hutton, Carrick and Nicholson, as well as Lumb, at a cost of 15 runs. He bowled straight and on a length, maintaining ruthless pressure and three of his victims were bowled.

None of the Durham bowlers wavered. Yorkshire were reduced to 49 for 5 and although Colin Johnson batted with determination, they never fully recovered and were all out in the fifty-ninth over for a meagre 135.

All that remained now was to see if Durham could keep their nerve. They were chasing a small target that made no demands for heroics or wild hitting. 'Stay there and the runs will come' was the philosophy.

The heaviest responsibility lay on the shoulders of Steve Atkinson and Inglis. Nicholson and Chris Old tested them with fiery pace and late movement that often had them groping, but they survived. They adopted the lesson taught by the great Yorkshireman Herbert Sutcliffe that if you are beaten by a good ball, you simply shape up for the next one and forget the escape you have just had. Grit and determination were the qualities of the opening stand and when Steve Atkinson was caught and bowled by Carrick the partnership was worth 58 and Durham were on their way to victory.

Inglis also fell to Carrick for a splendid 47 with the total at 63. Greensword now took over the anchor role, but he never missed an opportunity to punish the loose ball. March was run out at 87 and Alan Old was caught behind nine runs later. This was a crucial period for Durham, but the left-handed Neil Riddell stayed while 27 were scored and when he was bowled by Nicholson the minor county were in touching distance of the winning tape.

In fact, Soakell scored 10 of the final 15 runs scored, finishing with a final flourish four off Nicholson. David had slain Goliath. For the first time in the history of the competition a minor county had beaten one of the seniors, and the giant to fall had been the greatest prize of all — Yorkshire.

Not surprisingly, Brian Lander, as captain and bowler, was named Man-of-the-Match. For him and for his side, it was a memorable day.

Durham received a special award of £200 from the Gillette company to help them in their celebrations. They progressed no further in the competition, Essex beating them by seven wickets at Chester-le-Street in the next round, but nobody will ever take away their day of glory, nor will anyone forget that they were the first minor county to triumph over senior opponents.

YORKSHIRE *v* DURHAM
Gillette Cup, Round One
at Harrogate
30 June 1973

Yorkshire

G. Boycott (capt)	b Wilkinson	14
R.G. Lumb	c Old, b Lander	4
P.J. Sharpe	c Cole, b Inglis	12
J.H. Hampshire	c Inglis, b Lander	10
C. Johnson	hit wkt, b Greensword	44
R.A. Hutton	b Lander	0
C.M. Old	b March	5
* D.L. Bairstow	lbw, b Greensword	11
P. Carrick	b Lander	18
H.P. Cooper	not out	10
A.G. Nicholson	b Lander	0
Extras	b 1, lb 6	7
		135

	O	M	R	W
Wilkinson	12	3	33	1
Old	7	2	10	—
Lander	11.4	3	15	5
Inglis	8	3	23	1
March	8	3	18	1
Greensword	12	2	29	2

fall of wickets
1—18, 2—32, 3—34, 4—49, 5—49, 6—80, 7—100, 8—121, 9—135

Durham
R. Inglis	c Cooper, b Carrick	47
S.R. Atkinson	c and b Carrick	14
S. Greensword	not out	35
J.G. March	run out	7
A.G.B. Old	c Bairstow, b Cooper	6
N.A. Riddell	b Nicholson	15
D.W. Soakell	not out	10
P.J. Crane		
B.R. Lander (capt)		
J.S. Wilkinson		
* R. Cole		
Extras	lb 4	4
	(for 5 wkts)	138

	O	M	R	W
Old	8	1	15	—
Nicholson	11.3	3	27	1
Cooper	12	3	25	1
Carrick	12	4	32	2
Hutton	8	1	35	—

fall of wickets
1—58, 2—63, 3—87, 4—96, 5—123

Durham won by 5 wickets

ENGLAND v WEST INDIES

PRUDENTIAL TROPHY

At Headingley

5 September 1973

When the West Indies came to England in 1973 they had not won a Test match for seven years, during which time they had played twenty Tests. 1973 saw the beginning of the West Indian revival which was to carry them to supremacy in the world of cricket for the next decade. Of the three Test matches played that summer the one at Edgbaston was drawn, but West Indies totally outplayed England at Lord's and The Oval.

The game at The Oval saw West Indies victorious by 158 runs. At Lord's they scored a thrilling 652 for 8 declared and bowled England out for 233 and 193. Nine days after the Lord's Test came the first of the Prudential Trophy matches. England were at a very low ebb.

The crushing defeat at Lord's had been Ray Illingworth's last game for England. He was succeeded by Mike Denness, captain of Kent, who had not played in the series against the West Indies. There were other new faces in the team for the one-day international. Mike Smith of Middlesex, never to play a Test match, Chris Old, Bob Taylor and Mike Hendrick replaced Amiss, Luckhurst, Knott and Arnold.

There was early success for England to encourage the new captain. In the third over, with only four runs scored, Roy Fredericks edged Willis to slip and Greig's large hands cupped the ball with ease.

Foster took some time to find his touch, but Kanhai was in sparkling form and when Foster was out at 65 he and Clive Lloyd threatened to savage the England attack much as they, Sobers and Julien had done at Lord's.

With the score at 115 Kanhai drove Underwood high to long-on where Greig took a splendid catch on the run, but West Indies went to lunch at 122 for 3 from thirty-two overs and England's prospects looked no brighter than they had done after two days of the Lord's Test. With Lloyd in fine form and Sobers, Kallicharran, Boyce and Julien still to establish themselves, a huge West Indian total seemed inevitable.

In the afternoon the game changed dramatically. Clive Lloyd aimed a great, cross-batted swipe at Willis and had his off stump knocked out of the ground, a silly shot. 132 for 4.

The thirty-fifth over was bowled by Chris Old and it was the most vital over of the game for England. Gary Sobers was caught behind by Taylor for nought and the roar had scarcely died down when Bernard Julian suffered the same fate second ball. 133 for 6.

Alvin Kallicharran was not at his best, but he survived and kept the score moving. Then came another decisive over. Underwood bowled a quicker ball down the leg side which beat Kallicharran and Taylor stumped him quite brilliantly.

The Derbyshire wicket-keeper had been kept out of the Test team by Knott's superior batting, but few would argue that he was not the best wicket-keeper in the world. A quiet, kindly man who breathes efficiency and technical perfection, Bob Taylor must rank as one of the very greatest and most accomplished of England keepers and it is ludicrous that he has not represented his country more often.

The West Indies had not recovered from Taylor's superb piece of work before, in the same over and only one run later, Underwood bowled the dangerous Boyce with a yorker. So, with only nine overs left, the West Indies found themselves, bewilderingly, at 159 for 8.

Deryck Murray salvaged what he could from the wreck with some able assistance from Vanburn Holder. They added 22 runs in eight overs before Holder fell to Mike Hendrick and Murray was run out off the last ball of the same over. Seven wickets had fallen for 59 runs in the twenty overs since lunch and an England victory was now a possibility, albeit that their tail was long.

Dreams of victory were quickly broken when Boycott was caught at first slip in the third over. Boycott had been unwell after the Lord's Test, but he felt a responsibility to appear in this match in front of his own Yorkshire crowd. His duck was a bitter disappointment. His three-year self-imposed exile from Test cricket was only a year away.

Mike Denness came to the wicket as captain of England for

the first time with the score at 3 for 1. How unkindly history treats some men. It has stamped Mike Denness as the captain who lost the series to the Australia of Lillee and Thomson in their heyday. It has recorded him as the England captain who left himself out of the side in the same series because he was not scoring runs. It tells of him as the captain who left Kent in unfriendly circumstances, forgetting that he led them to three John Player League titles, victory in the Benson and Hedges Cup twice and the Gillette Cup in 1974. An intelligent and sensitive man of great courage and integrity, he faced the greatest of challenges in his first visit to the crease as England's captain. A Yorkshire crowd is, perhaps, not the ideal backing for an England captain who comes from the south, even if he was born in Scotland.

Partnering Denness was Mike Smith, a reliable opening bat for Middlesex whom the selectors treated disgracefully, calling him up at a late hour to join the England party for a final Test match and then neither playing him nor including him in the group of seventeen to go on tour a few weeks later. These two faced the job of repairing the England innings with great determination. Runs were essential, but it was just as essential not to lose another wicket.

In twenty-two overs they added 71 and the England innings had just the foundation that it needed for victory. Then they faltered.

It was the incomparable Lance Gibbs who restricted the flow of England runs in an economical spell and it was Julien and Holder who removed Hayes and Fletcher so that three wickets fell in the space of ten overs while only 21 runs were scored. 95 for 4 and England struggling.

They would have been struggling more had Gary Sobers caught Tony Greig low down at first slip when the future England captain had scored only twelve. Greig and Denness were the last of the recognised English batsmen so that much depended on them. They had to survive and they had to score runs quickly. They did both. In nine overs they added 48 and then Mike Denness's fine innings came to an end.

He had batted for under two and a half hours and scored 66 off forty-one overs. It was an innings of resource and initiative and no little courage, and it made an England victory possible for when he was bowled trying to sweep Gibbs only 39 were needed in ten overs. With five wickets remaining this did not seem too arduous a task.

The quality of the rest of the batting was doubtful, however, and much depended on Tony Greig. Chris Old stayed while 14 were added and Taylor was run out after another 14 were put on.

When the fifty-fourth over began, Keith Boyce bowling, England needed 7 to win with three wickets in hand. One run was scored and then Greig attempted a big hit, but he succeeded only in skying the ball to cover where the safe hands of Sobers compensated for the earlier miss. The batsmen had crossed as the catch was being made and Mike Hendrick was bowled next ball. Derek Underwood saved the hat-trick and the last over arrived with England needing four to win and the last pair at the wicket.

Gary Sobers bowled the last over. His first ball produced nothing, but Bob Willis swung at the next ball and hit it high back over the bowler's head for two. The third ball of the over was edged down to third man for two and England had won by one wicket with three balls to spare.

It was a momentous victory for England at a time when her cricket was in a traumatic state. When you have just been beaten by an innings and 226 runs in a Test match, victory in a one-day international against the same opponents is a very welcome crumb of comfort.

Mike Denness was applauded as the hero of the day and Bill Bowes, the great Yorkshire fast bowler, named him Man-of-the-Match. It was a memorable start for the new England skipper, a fine personal achievement which was an inspiration to his side. It was something for him to reflect upon in the less sunny days which came later.

ENGLAND *v* WEST INDIES
Prudential Trophy
at Headingley
5 September 1973

West Indies

R.C. Fredericks	c Greig, b Willis	4
M.L.C. Foster	c Greig, b Old	25
R.B. Kanhai (capt)	c Greig, b Underwood	55
C.H. Lloyd	b Willis	31
A.I. Kallicharran	st Taylor, b Underwood	26
G.S. Sobers	c Taylor, b Old	0
B.D. Julien	c Taylor, b Old	0
K.D. Boyce	b Underwood	7
* D.L. Murray	run out	11
V.A. Holder	c Old, b Hendrick	10
L.R. Gibbs	not out	0
Extras	lb 12	12
		181

	O	M	R	W
Willis	10	2	29	2
Hendrick	11	4	27	1
Old	11	1	43	3
Underwood	11	2	30	3
Greig	11	—	40	—

fall of wickets
1—4, 2—65, 3—115, 4—132, 5—133, 6—133, 7—158, 8—159, 9—181

England

G. Boycott	c Kanhai, b Holder	0
M.J. Smith	lbw, b Julien	31
M.H. Denness (capt)	b Gibbs	66
F.C. Hayes	c Murray, b Julien	9
K.W.R. Fletcher	lbw, b Holder	2
A.W. Greig	c Sobers, b Boyce	48
C.M. Old	b Sobers	4
* R.W. Taylor	run out	8
M. Hendrick	b Boyce	1
R.G.D. Willis	not out	5
D.L. Underwood	not out	1
Extras	b 1, lb 3, nb 3	7
	(for 9 wkts)	182

	O	M	R	W
Sobers	10.3	3	31	1
Holder	11	1	34	2
Boyce	11	1	40	2
Julien	11	1	40	2
Gibbs	11	—	30	1

fall of wickets
1—3, 2—74, 3—93, 4—95, 5—143, 6—157, 7—171, 8—176, 9—176

England won by 1 wicket

AUSTRALIA v WEST INDIES

PRUDENTIAL WORLD CUP FINAL

At Lord's

21 June 1975

The first limited-over encounters at international level could not be considered a success. Generous sponsorship by the Prudential Company had not received the response in commitment that it deserved.

Beginning in 1972, England had met the touring sides in fifty-five over matches for the Prudential Trophy. These games were scheduled to follow Test matches and initially they were memorable only for their weariness and lack of involvement, qualities which did not suggest that they would survive as an integral part of the international cricket fixture list.

It was with some scepticism therefore that the news of the first Prudential World Cup in 1975 was received. The idea of a world cup competition between the cricketing nations had long been mooted, but, hitherto, finance, structure and venue had seemed to pose insurmountable problems. Now the generous Prudential Assurance Company provided the financial backing, the Gillette Cup gave credibility to structure and the cancellation of South Africa's scheduled tour of England created the venue.

The competition was blessed with a month of glorious weather. England and New Zealand qualified for the semi-finals from Group A, the West Indies and Australia from Group B.

Group B was by far the stronger group with Sri Lanka, pointless, but giving a brave indication of their worth, and the formidable Pakistani side being the non-qualifiers. The meeting between the West Indies and Australia at The Oval had seen the Australians outplayed in every phase of the game.

The semi-finals brought together Australia and England, and West Indies and New Zealand. On a dreadful wicket at Headingley, England collapsed to Gary Gilmour, 6 for 14, and were out for 93. Australia were reduced to 39 for 6, but Gilmour proved as effective with the bat as he had been with the ball, and scored 28 not out to steer Australia into the final against West Indies, easy winners over New Zealand at The Oval.

Saturday, 21 June: the longest day of the year and one of the longest and most glorious days in cricket history.

Throughout the competition West Indies had batted second, Clive Lloyd asking the opposition to bat whenever he won the toss. But this time Ian Chappell won the toss and invited the West Indies to bat first, probably reasoning that it was what they would like doing least.

Whatever his real reasons, the Australian captain's decision met with quick success. Gilmour had bowled three no-balls in the opening over, much to the noisy delight of the West Indian contingent near the tavern, but then, with 12 runs on the board, Roy Fredericks, who had savaged Lillee and Thomson at The Oval, hooked a Lillee bouncer over the boundary at long-leg, but lost his balance and fell on his wicket.

Kallicharran, too, had batted splendidly in the previous match with Australia and he again began confidently, but he cut unwisely at a ball from Gilmour and was caught behind. Greenidge was totally unable to capture his usual exciting form and after eighty minutes of ineffective groping he edged a slower ball from Thomson low to Marsh. 50 for 3 and Clive Lloyd now joined Kanhai.

The West Indies captain had had little chance of showing any sort of form on his side's journey to the final; most of the time he had not been needed. Now a big innings from him was essential.

There are few cricketers who look less likely to score runs when they come to the wicket than Clive Lloyd. The dragging feet, the slight stoop, the spectacles, the seemingly small bat in the big hand, all give indication of a man whose size is beyond his control and who would rather be in bed. We are deceived. It is not a drag of the feet, but a slink. He is not stooping, but waiting to pounce. Bat and man will become one in a display of power and fluent movement.

Ian Chappell brought Lillee back into the attack to test Lloyd. Almost immediately the West Indian captain hooked Lillee, mightily and majestically, square for six. He drove Walker through the covers off the back foot with an ease that denied the power of the shot. The onslaught had begun.

Rohan Kanhai accepted the responsible and uncharacteristic role of anchor man. For eleven overs he did not score, but he gave Lloyd exactly the support that was needed in the circumstances.

Lloyd was at his blistering best and Lord's rang to the sound of his bat; joy in the sun.

In thirty-six overs they added 149. Lloyd reached one of the most brilliantly exciting and inevitable hundreds ever seen at Lord's. In venue, occasion and execution it was in perfect context. He batted for 108 minutes and received eighty-two balls in making his hundred. Beside his two sixes he hit twelve fours.

His innings ended on a controversial note. He was given out caught behind down the leg-side and showed a certain annoyance at the decision. The bowler was Gilmour who had returned for an economical spell in which he also took the wickets of Kanhai and Richards so that West Indies were 209 for 6 in the forty-sixth over and Australia hoped again.

But the platform was now firm for the temperament and technique of Boyce and Julien and they engaged in a whirlwind stand of 52. Boyce had an all too brief Test career. He reached the international level later than most, but he was perfectly suited to the one-day game and he shared with Sobers and Lloyd the ability to give the impression of a spring uncoiling.

With Deryck Murray, no mean batsman, as low as number nine, the West Indies were a formidable proposition for any attack as the last overs were bowled. 291 for 8 was the final score so that Australia were asked to score at a rate of nearly five runs an over and to set a record for the competition if they were to win.

It was not simply the speed at which the runs had to be scored that made this a difficult task, but the sheer number of runs that had to be obtained. No side hopes to begin to score at five or six an over, but when nearly three hundred runs are needed it is imperative that as many as possible are scored early on or the weight of responsibility on the later batsmen will be too great.

It was this pressure to score quickly too soon that threw the Australians into trouble. Turner suggested authority, but McCosker was fretting across the line, looking for runs. With the score at 25 he tried to work the ball through mid-wicket, but it was Boyce's away swinger and the ball found the edge and was well taken, low down, at second slip by Kallicharran.

Turner batted solidly and effectively and with Ian Chappell quickly assured, runs came briskly. There were signs that the West Indies would have a real fight on their hands, but suddenly, and inexplicably, a corporate madness gripped the Australian batsmen.

Runs had been coming at a good rate and it was surprising therefore that there should be an agitation that they should come more quickly, but, within a short space of time, Turner and the Chappell brothers were all run out in going for inadvisable runs.

A complete misunderstanding left Turner scampering for safety, but Richards hit the stumps with an underarm throw and Australia were 81 for 2. The Chappells then put on 34 with growing certainty. Ian Chappell pushed the ball out square on the off-side and the batsmen went for the run. Richards, throwing on the turn, hit the one stump visible to him and Greg Chappell was out. 115 for 3.

The unkindest cut of all, and the silliest, was the dismissal of Ian Chappell. With a century seemingly his for the taking, he hesitated over a third run as Richards misfielded the ball and was then left stranded as the ball was returned to the bowler, Lloyd, who broke the wicket.

The loss of the Chappells was a grave blow to Australia and the West Indies, exhilarating in the field, sensed victory. At 162 for 4, Australia needed 130 runs from the last twenty-two overs.

There were some elegant shots from Doug Walters, but once more he failed to demonstrate his true worth to an English public. Marsh flurried briefly and 76 runs were needed off ten overs with four wickets standing.

A fine mid-innings spell from Keith Boyce accounted for Marsh, Edwards and Gilmour. Ross Edwards played a pleasant miniature and then skied the ball as did the dangerous Gilmour. Max Walker ran himself out and Australia were 233 for 9 with one ball of the fifty-third over left when Jeff Thomson was joined by Dennis Lillee. Fifty-nine runs were needed and only forty-three balls in which to get them, numbers ten and eleven at the wicket. West Indies, one imagined, had already captured the World Cup.

The partnership of Lillee and Thomson, the fast bowlers, has struck a chord of terror in many a batsman and not a few spectators. They breathe hostility. They sweep batsmen aside as Tamburlaine swept aside opposing hordes. There is in their bowling that indestructable quality that can be neither taught nor given, the unwillingness to admit defeat. From the fire of their bowling they now summoned qualities of aggression to their batting and for a few moments it seemed as though Australia would win.

These two mighty men threw their bats with such force that even when they did not hit the ball with the middle of the bat, they still cleared the field. The West Indies were forced back to the boundary, conceding the singles. There were some fierce and authentic drives, and there were some narrow escapes, but the score mounted.

Twenty-one runs were needed from two overs. An impossible task suddenly looked as if it would be accomplished in one ball from a most bizarre incident.

Holder bowled a no-ball which Thomson skied to Roy Fredericks at cover. Fredericks threw at the bowler's wicket in an attempt to run the batsman out. The ball missed the wicket and with no one backing up went for overthrows which Lillee and Thomson gleefully accepted.

In the constant roar that was issuing from the excited crowd few heard the call of no-ball and, believing that when Fredericks caught Thomson the West Indies had won, thousands swarmed onto the pitch. Fielders were knocked over and the ball was lost from sight as in the middle of the arena Lillee and Thomson tore up and down. The umpires called 'dead ball'. The crowds were ushered off and 3 runs were added to the score.

Lillee and Thomson had added 41 runs. Nine balls remained and 18 runs were required for victory. It was three minutes short of a quarter to nine and Lord's was a cauldron of excitement. And then came the last great irony.

Thomson played and missed, and the ball went through to Murray. Believing that his partner was prepared to take a bye to the wicket-keeper, Thomson charged up the wicket. Lillee sent him back. Diving in the dust, Thomson was some six inches out as Murray threw down the wicket. In the craving for runs, Thomson became the *fifth* Australian batsman to be run out.

The field and the players are swamped with happy crowds. Clive Lloyd holds the cup on high. West Indies — and cricket — have won.

As Norman Preston wrote later, 'The game has never produced better entertainment in one day.' It was a game, he said, 'that those who were there and the millions who watched it on television will never forget.'

At its first attempt the Prudential World Cup had become firmly established.

AUSTRALIA *v* WEST INDIES
Prudential World Cup Final
at Lord's
21 June 1975

West Indies		
R.C. Fredericks	hit wkt, b Lillee	7
C.G. Greenidge	c Marsh, b Thomson	13
A.I. Kallicharran	c Marsh, b Gilmour	12
R.B. Kanhai	b Gilmour	55
C.H. Lloyd (capt)	c Marsh, b Gilmour	102
I.V.A. Richards	b Gilmour	5
K.D. Boyce	c G.S. Chappell, b Thomson	34
B.D. Julien	not out	26
*D.L. Murray	c and b Gilmour	14
V.A. Holder	not out	6
A.M.E Roberts		
Extras	lb 6, nb 11	17
	(for 8 wkts)	291

	O	M	R	W
Lillee	12	1	55	1
Gilmour	12	2	48	5
Thomson	12	1	44	2
Walker	12	1	71	—
G.S. Chappell	7	—	33	—
Walters	5	—	23	—

fall of wickets
1—12, 2—27, 3—50, 4—199, 5—206, 6—209, 7—261, 8—285

Australia

A. Turner	run out	40
R.B. McCosker	c Kallicharran, b Boyce	7
I.M. Chappell (capt)	run out	62
G.S. Chappell	run out	15
K.D. Walters	b Lloyd	35
* R.W. Marsh	b Boyce	11
R. Edwards	c Fredericks, b Boyce	28
G.J. Gilmour	c Kanhai, b Boyce	14
M.H.N. Walker	run out	7
J.R. Thomson	run out	21
D.K. Lillee	not out	16
Extras	b 2, lb 9, nb 7	18
		274

	O	M	R	W
Julien	12	–	58	–
Roberts	11	1	45	–
Boyce	12	–	50	4
Holder	11.4	1	65	–
Lloyd	12	1	38	1

fall of wickets
1–25, 2–81, 3–115, 4–162, 5–170, 6–195, 7–221, 8–231, 9–233

West Indies won by 17 runs

KENT v WORCESTERSHIRE

BENSON AND HEDGES CUP FINAL

At Lord's

17 July 1976

Adversity often wins an acclaim that is not granted to success. Heroic failure achieves a renown that is not accorded to remorseless victory. The Olympic Games Marathon of 1908 has passed into history as the 'Dorando Marathon'. Dorando Pietri was an Italian sweet-maker who collapsed when yards from the finishing line of the marathon. An official stepped forward and helped him over the line. This natural and humane act earned Dorando Pietri disqualification and cost him the gold medal he had earned. Nevertheless, the name of the winner, Hayes of America, has been forgotten by all but the most ardent students of the history of athletics. The name of Dorando, the Christian name which was wrongly printed as his surname on the programme, has become part of sporting legend.

The Benson and Hedges Cup final of 1976 has become known as the D'Oliveira final. It was, in fact, won by Kent and Graham Johnson was Man-of-the-Match.

This was the fifth Benson and Hedges Cup final and it was Kent's second victory. Under the leadership of Mike Denness they had maintained their record as one of the very best sides in the country, capable of winning any, or all, of the four major competitions. In fact, from 1970 to 1978 they won at least one trophy every season with the exception of 1971 and 1975, and in the first of those seasons they were Gillette Cup finalists and in the second they were third in the John Player League.

By 1976, Worcestershire's great days were just behind them. They had been county champions in 1974 and had won the John Player League in 1971. They had reached the final of the Benson and Hedges Cup in 1973 when they had been beaten by Kent by 39 runs in a most exciting match. Kent were favoured to repeat their win when the two teams reached the final of the 1976 competition.

Norman Gifford won the toss and asked Kent to bat. Putting
the other side in to bat has become something of a tradition in the
one-day game, but one still doubts the wisdom of it, and on this
occasion Gifford must have doubted the sagacity of his decision.

It is true that Graham Johnson began most uncertainly
against the bowling of Imran Khan and John Inchmore, but
Woolmer was quickly into his stride. In his early years Woolmer
had looked a most aggressive, pugnacious batsman. As he
matured he sacrificed strokes for solidity and he became an
England player who never revealed to a wider public the exciting
range of shots of which he had suggested he was capable in
those first years with Kent.

In the context of the limited-over game he was able to play
with more adventure and his driving was particularly powerful
and, taking the ball off his toes, he forced it square on the leg-
side to great effect. Johnson had now overcome all uncertainty
and runs began to flow.

The opening bowlers retired wicketless and Pridgeon and
D'Oliveira joined the attack. D'Oliveira is a particularly difficult
bowler to attack and although he may not pose the greatest of
problems if one is content on survival, he is very restrictive
when one is intent on scoring quickly. Initially he curtailed the
scoring, but then Woolmer attacked him ferociously, attaining
fifteen from an over.

Almost immediately, following a wild piece of throwing,
D'Oliveira chased after the ball and tore a hamstring. He was
helped from the field and, only with assistance, could he climb
the stairs to the dressing room. There the leg was packed around
with ice, but the doctors declared that the injury was so severe
that he would be unable to bat.

In the thirtieth over Woolmer drove Gifford high to deep
mid-on where Inchmore took the catch. Woolmer had scored 61
out of 110, the first three-figured opening partnership in a one-
day final at Lord's.

Deprived of a key bowler, Worcestershire were quick to
resort to defence. Denness was caught behind off Inchmore
after a brisk stand, but from the thirty-seventh over onwards
Gifford adopted a purely defensive field. The Worcestershire
players ringed the boundary and for the next fifteen overs they
prevented a four from being scored.

In the forty-fourth over Johnson was bowled by Boyns who had responded well to the added responsibility thrust upon him by D'Oliveira's injury. Johnson's had been a fine innings. When he left, Kent were 171 for 3 with some brisk scorers to exploit the last eleven overs.

In response to Gifford's defensive field, Asif Iqbal and Alan Ealham concentrated on swift running and there can have been few better run stealers than these two. It was the fifty-second over before Asif beat the ring of fielders to reach the boundary, but runs came at six an over for the last ten of the innings.

Kent's 236 was the highest made in a Benson and Hedges final at that time although it has twice been beaten since. The score still looked attainable provided the Worcestershire stars like Glenn Turner and Imran Khan could produce their usual form and provided that D'Oliveira could bat. Few in the crowd knew that medical advice decreed that he should not bat.

Turner and Ormrod began briskly against Jarvis and Asif and runs came at three an over. Shepherd and Woolmer were brought on and Shepherd immediately struck a full length.

In the thirteenth over Shepherd struck the vital blow. He moved the ball away off the seam, found the outside edge of Turner's bat and Knott took a splendid catch low to his right in the first slip position.

D'Oliveira should have come in at number three, but Phil Neale was promoted because of D'Oliveira's injury. Neale found the task of scoring briskly a very difficult one and he laboured until he fell to a good catch at cover when he lashed out at Shepherd.

Ormrod continued to play well but Underwood joined the attack and Worcestershire crumbled.

Derek Underwood is the meanest of bowlers in limited-over cricket and now he adopted the policy of attacking on or just outside the leg-stump.

Ormrod, Imran Khan and Hemsley attempted to counter this form of attack by hooking and all fell the same way. Swinging Underwood high to the area between square- and long-leg, they were caught in quick succession by Graham Johnson who was positioned on the boundary rope. Each catch was beautifully judged and Johnson's feat in taking four catches as well as scoring a fine 78 deservedly won him the gold award.

While Underwood and Johnson were doing their double act there was a great deal of activity in the Worcestershire dressing room. Norman Gifford had pleaded with the medical experts to allow D'Oliveira to bat, but they had said that it was out of the question. Now, with the game slipping away from Worcestershire, he appealed to the doctors again and to D'Oliveira himself.

D'Oliveira's whole life has been founded on courage and dignity and this was a challenge fitting to the man. It was decided that the whole of his left leg would have to be strapped to try to prevent it from having any feeling at all, not even in the toes. There was a roar of appreciation from the crowd when, at the fall of the fourth wicket, D'Oliveira hobbled down the pavilion steps with Glenn Turner, who was to act as runner, walking by his side.

The Worcestershire score was 90 for 4 from thirty-three overs when D'Oliveira came to the wicket. He could only stand firm footed at the crease and relied mainly on powerful short arm jabs. He has recorded his strategy in his autobiography, *Time to Declare*: 'I decided to get as far over to the off-stump as I could and then give it a slog on the leg-side. I wanted to hit Derek Underwood over extra cover's head if I could, so I just stood there and carved. My left leg was giving me agony and I could only play off my back foot; I dreaded getting a bouncer because I wouldn't have had a hope of avoiding it. I took middle and off guard so that I didn't have to worry too much about footwork; if I missed a straight one, I was out, simple as that. I kept my left foot slightly off the ground and hit through the line of the ball whenever it came near me. My power and the fact that I was a back-foot player obviously helped me.'

Boyns gave D'Oliveira valuable assistance and the Worcestershire run rate increased as D'Oliveira bludgeoned and carved a succession of fours. Once he hit Richard Hills on the rise and sent the ball soaring over mid-off into the pavilion seats for six. Worcestershire needed 75 from the last ten overs and if D'Oliveira could maintain this powerful hitting, the task would be accomplished, but in the forty-seventh over he lashed out once too often and was bowled by Jarvis. Kent were mightily relieved as they turned and clapped D'Oliveira all the way back to the pavilion. The reception that he received was one fitting a hero. He had scored 50 out of 76 in fourteen overs.

The big guns of Gifford and Inchmore did not fire that day and Worcestershire lasted just over five overs after D'Oliveira's dismissal so that they were beaten in a Lord's final for the fourth time.

Mike Denness held the cup aloft and Graham Johnson received his gold medal from Sir Gary Sobers. Kent supporters rejoiced at another triumph and rightly so, but the 1976 Benson and Hedges Cup final will always be best remembered for the heroic fifty scored by the injured Basil D'Oliveira.

KENT *v* WORCESTERSHIRE
Benson and Hedges Cup Final
at Lord's
17 July 1976

Kent

G.W. Johnson	b Boyns	78
R.A. Woolmer	c Inchmore, b Gifford	61
M.H. Denness (capt)	c Wilcock, b Inchmore	15
Asif Iqbal	not out	48
A.G.E. Ealham	c Ormrod, b Boyns	11
J.N. Shepherd	c Boyns, b Gifford	8
*A.P.E. Knott	b Imran Khan	1
C.J.C. Rowe	run out	0
R.W. Hills		
D.L. Underwood		
K.B.S. Jarvis		
Extras	b 2, lb 10, nb 2	14
	(for 7 wkts)	236

	O	M	R	W
Imran Khan	9	1	26	1
Inchmore	11	—	57	1
Pridgeon	9	1	35	—
D'Oliveira	4	1	21	—
Gifford	11	3	38	2
Boyns	11	—	45	2

fall of wickets
1—110, 2—155, 3—171, 4—194, 5—215, 6—220, 7—236

Worcestershire

J.A. Ormrod	c Johnson, b Underwood	37
G.M. Turner	c Knott, b Shepherd	14
P.A. Neale	c Johnson, b Shepherd	5
Imran Khan	c Johnson, b Underwood	12
E.J.O. Hemsley	c Johnson, b Underwood	15
B.L. D'Oliveira	b Jarvis	50
C.N. Boyns	c Knott, b Jarvis	15
* H.G. Wilcock	not out	19
N. Gifford (capt)	c Knott, b Jarvis	0
J.D. Inchmore	c Underwood, b Asif Iqbal	2
A.P. Pridgeon	b Jarvis	8
Extras	b 1, lb 12, w 1, nb 2	16
		193

	O	M	R	W
Jarvis	10.4	2	34	4
Asif Iqbal	9	—	35	1
Shepherd	7	—	17	2
Woolmer	11	3	27	—
Underwood	9	2	31	3
Hills	6	—	33	—

fall of wickets
1—40, 2—52, 3—70, 4—90, 5—126, 6—161, 7—166, 8—172, 9—175

Kent won by 43 runs

NORTHAMPTONSHIRE v LANCASHIRE

GILLETTE CUP FINAL

At Lord's

4 September 1976

In the years before the Second World War, Northamptonshire cricket became something of a joke. There were several fine players with the county in the thirties like Vallance Jupp, 'Nobby' Clark, Arnold Bakewell, whose career was tragically cut short by a road accident, and John Timms, but the county rarely rose above the last two places in the table. It became hard to recall that they had been runners-up in 1912.

After the Second World War there was a great change in fortune. Dennis Brookes had matured into a fine batsman. Freddie Brown joined the side as captain and went on to lead England. There were other imports in Tribe and Manning and, of course, there were Frank Tyson and Colin Milburn. In 1957 and 1965 they were runners-up in the County Championship, but still honour eluded them.

It must be admitted that home-grown players were still in short supply, but by 1976 they had gathered a group of players who were challenging for the county title and who reached the final of the Gillette Cup where they were to meet Lancashire.

Lancashire were the holders and were very much favourites to retain the trophy, but, in fact, the great days of Lancashire's limited-over success were drawing to a close.

The Lancashire path to the final had been strewn with convincing victories: Northants had won a narrow victory over Nottinghamshire in the second round and an equally narrow victory over Hampshire in the semi-final. Both experience and form pointed to a Lancashire triumph once more.

The weather had been kind to the Gillette Cup competition throughout the summer and Saturday, 4 September was no exception. Lancashire had not been able to call upon Clive Lloyd for the entire summer as he was captaining the West Indian side which was touring England and his absence obviously weakened the side. There was further discomfort when Mushtaq Mohammad won the toss and asked them to bat, for Lancashire, it was well known, were always happier when chasing runs.

There was a suggestion that the Lord's wicket might give some help to the seamers and this was certainly proved true as the day wore on. It was not the pitch, however, which was to blame for Lancashire's dismal start, but some fine Northants bowling.

Sarfraz Nawaz began with a maiden and then John Dye completely deceived Engineer with an in-swinging yorker and Lancashire were 0 for 1. The effect that this wicket had on the Northants side in general and on Dye himself was quite remarkable. The stocky, left-arm, medium pace bowler had spent nine years with Kent and was now in his fourth season with Northants for whom he was to play for just one more season after this final. He was always an underrated player, but rarely can he have bowled better than he did on that September morning in 1976. He made the ball lift disconcertingly from a length and not only did he make run scoring extremely difficult, he also looked as if he were about to take a wicket with every ball he bowled.

However, it was Sarfraz who dismissed Pilling, and Hodgson who caught and bowled Hayes well, but in the meantime Dye had delivered a crucial, if unintentional, blow to Lancashire's hopes. He made a ball lift sharply off a length and Wood, always susceptible with his grip, was struck on the right hand. He was in obvious pain and was led from the field. A bone had been chipped and he took no further part in the match which meant that Lancashire were not only losing an opening batsman, but also the man to whom they looked as one of their five bowlers.

At 45 for 3, with Wood unable to continue, Lancashire were in great trouble. They were saved from further humiliation by the two left-handers, skipper David Lloyd and the young South African John Abrahams who would probably not have been playing had Clive Lloyd been available. They batted with great good sense, never losing an opportunity to score against some tight bowling and added 95.

It was during this partnership that Mushtaq's captaincy was brought into question. Dye and Hodgson, who had bowled very well, both had overs in hand. The great Bishen Bedi had not yet delivered a ball, and all this while the makeshift bowlers, Larkins and Willey, were bowling their full complement of overs without taking a wicket and without looking like taking a wicket.

It was not until the fortieth over of the innings that Bedi was brought into the attack. Ah, Bishen Bedi, what a joy was there! Those who never saw this man bowl missed one of the very greatest aesthetic pleasures that cricket ever had to offer. It was the subtlety, the variety, the sheer magic of the man that delighted. He was a manifestation of intelligence solving a difficult mathematical problem. It was not simply that he spun the ball, and this he could control to his need, but that he manipulated his point of delivery so that, although always releasing the ball from near the highest point, his subtleties of change in the actual moment when he delivered the ball brought him a variety of flights and loop which none has bettered. The balance was perfect and his cunning a delight. The physical and the mental were fused at the vital moment, and this was the essence of his beauty.

He quickly bowled both David Lloyd and Abrahams when they tried to attack him and Lancashire were 143 for 5, and Barry Wood at the hospital.

Sarfraz returned for his final flourish and bowled Jack Simmons and nine runs later Bedi had his third victim when he had Ratcliffe, anxious to hit, caught by Larkins.

After fifty-nine overs Lancashire stood at 169 for 7 and Northants had the game as good as won.

Mushtaq Mohammad has been severely criticised for what happened next although at the time there were few who disagreed with what he did. David Hughes was 13 not out, Peter Lever was 8 not out. Hughes' onslaught on John Mortimore was five years in the past and part of history. None thought that he would ever repeat the feat. After all he had scored only 295 runs for Lancashire that season at an average of 16.38. Those were not figures of which Northants, Bedi or Mushtaq should be frightened.

Bedi had sent down ten overs and taken three for 26, he had bowled as well as those figures suggest. Where Mushtaq had erred had been in delaying Bedi's entry into the attack until the fortieth over for what it meant now was that while Bedi could

confidently be entrusted with the last over, John Dye, the best
bowler on either side during the day, languished in the outfield
with five of his twelve overs unfulfilled. Hodgson, too, had six
overs that were never used, and yet these two men were the
most economical bowlers of the day. But it was Bedi who
bowled the last over.

Hughes' course of action was quite plain. He would attempt
to recapture the past and to score as many runs as possible from
the over. At least this time the light was good and Lancashire
still had a chance to win the match with their bowling whatever
he accomplished with the bat.

The first ball was crashed through the off-side field for four.
The next was swung high over mid-wicket for six and the crowd
erupted. History was being repeated.

Undeterred, applauding the batsman's efforts, Bedi looped
the ball into the air again. Once more Hughes swung hard and
two were scampered. Two more runs came off the next ball.

For one of the few occasions in his distinguished career, Bedi
responded to aggression with something close to a defensive
tactic. He pushed the ball through a little quicker and flatter.
Hughes anticipated and whisked it away over long-on for six.
Around the ground few people were left sitting.

Bedi moved in to bowl the last ball and in a final flourish
Hughes hoisted it over mid-wicket for the third six of the over.
Twenty-six runs had been scored off the over, two more than
Hughes had taken off Mortimore in that memorable over at Old
Trafford, and Lancashire had a fighting chance. Not only was
their score considerably more than had seemed possible earlier,
but they had ended their innings on a high note. The psycho-
logical advantage was theirs for the first time in the day.

The Lancashire opening bowling was good. Peter Lever was a
Test player and Peter Lee should have been one. An ex-Northants
seamer, Peter Lee was probably the most valuable bowler ever
to play in limited-over cricket and why he did not represent
England in a one-day international remains a mystery to this day.

The greatest threat to Northants, apart from these two, was
their own lack of confidence. They had had some terrible crises
of confidence on their way to the final and their supporters
feared one now. Roy Virgin, the former Somerset favourite, and
Peter Willey responded to the tension by digging in.

Once Willey hit Peter Lever for three fours in an over and Virgin came out of his shell to loft Hughes into the pavilion, but mostly it was solid stuff. It had to be. The going was slow, but a sound start was essential. The fireworks could come when the target was within easy reach.

What Northants feared was a repeat of what had happened in the semi-final at Southampton. There they had chased a target of 216 and had reached 180 with only three men out. Then they collapsed, losing five wickets for 31 runs. Victory came in the unlikely batting of Bishen Bedi who played a classic on-drive off John Rice on the penultimate ball of the last over to score the winning boundary. It was a superb shot, but Northants supporters did not wish to look to chance that it would be repeated.

Virgin and Willey put on 103 for the first wicket and Willey played the most assured innings of the day. He hit eleven fours and his cover driving was a delight. He looked impregnable. His batting had solidity and pugnacity, and he deservedly won the Man-of-the-Match award from Colin Cowdrey.

1976 was a strange year for Peter Willey. He was picked for England for the first time and in two Tests against the West Indies he made a most favourable impression, and then he played this fine knock in the Gillette final and England discarded him for four years.

When Virgin and Willey left, Northants stumbled. Mushtaq fretted too much. David Steele, who had been left out of the side in the semi-final and had been England's hero of the summer — his last in Test cricket — played a few important shots before providing Hughes with his one expensive wicket when he lofted him to Kennedy, fielding substitute for Barry Wood.

Both Larkins and Cook failed and Lee and Lever had now returned, threatening to take a stranglehold on the game and squeeze Northants to defeat at the very last.

It was wicket-keeper George Sharp who steadied the nerves. There were no histrionics, just sensible run gathering and with three overs left only eight runs were needed.

David Lloyd had been forced to throw Lever and Lee into the attack in an effort to snatch victory, but now their quotas were exhausted and it was Jack Simmons who came up to bowl the fifty-ninth over with the scores level.

Appropriately George Sharp struck the first ball for four and Northants, so long the Cinderellas of cricket, had at last arrived at the ball.

There was none who begrudged them this long-awaited success even if they had made a few hearts flutter on the way and given David Hughes the opportunity of playing yet another memorable 'one-over' innings.

NORTHAMPTONSHIRE *v* LANCASHIRE
Gillette Cup Final
at Lord's
4 September 1976

Lancashire

B. Wood	retired hurt	14
* F.M. Engineer	b Dye	0
H. Pilling	c Cook, b Sarfraz	3
F.C. Hayes	c and b Hodgson	19
D. Lloyd (capt)	b Bedi	48
J. Abrahams	c Bedi	46
D.P. Hughes	not out	39
J. Simmons	b Sarfraz	1
R.M. Ratcliffe	c Larkins, b Bedi	4
P. Lever	not out	8
P.G. Lee		
Extras	b 1, lb 9, w 2, nb 1	13
	(for 7 wkts)	195

	O	M	R	W
Sarfraz Nawaz	12	2	39	2
Dye	7	3	9	1
Hodgson	6	3	10	1
Larkins	12	4	31	—
Willey	12	2	41	—
Bedi	11	—	52	3

fall of wickets
1—0, 2—17, 3—45, 4—140, 5—143, 6—148, 7—157

Northamptonshire

R.T. Virgin	c and b Ratcliffe	53
P. Willey	c Engineer, b Lee	65
Mushtaq Mohammad (capt)	c Hayes, b Ratcliffe	13
D.S. Steele	c sub (Kennedy), b Hughes	24
W. Larkins	lbw, b Lever	8
G. Cook	c Engineer, b Lever	15
• G. Sharp	not out	10
Sarfraz Nawaz	not out	3
A. Hodgson		
B.S. Bedi		
J.C.J. Dye		
Extras	b 5, lb 1, nb 2	8
	(for 6 wkts)	199

	O	M	R	W
Lever	12	3	29	1
Lee	12	4	29	2
Simmons	11.1	2	29	–
Ratcliffe	12	2	48	2
Hughes	11	–	56	1

fall of wickets
1–103, 2–127, 3–143, 4–154, 5–178, 6–182

Northamptonshire won by 4 wickets

GLAMORGAN v SOMERSET

JOHN PLAYER LEAGUE

At Cardiff

5 September 1976

In many ways the cricket authorities were slow to capitalise on the success of the Gillette Cup for it was obvious that one-day cricket had an appeal to the spectators and was economically good for the game. There were others who were quicker to realise the financial gains to be made by instant cricket, and in the late nineteen-sixties, the Rothman Cavaliers, an exciting team of Test veterans like Denis Compton, Tom Graveney, Ted Dexter and Fred Trueman, toured the country and played Sunday matches before large crowds. Many of these games were televised. Large sums of money were raised and much of it was donated to the MCC.

It was apparent that there was an eager public waiting to watch cricket on Sundays. With sponsorship and television coverage here was a rich source of revenue for first-class cricket. The John Player League was born and a host of people who had never been to a first-class game, and who never would go to a first-class game, became Sunday afternoon addicts as they settled back in their armchairs after lunch and watched the forty-over matches.

There were teething troubles in that first year of 1969 and some teams and players took longer to adapt to the game than others, but in the years that followed the matches themselves were a tremendous success. Grounds bulged with spectators on Sunday afternoons and the size of the television audience grew week by week.

In the final weeks of the season excitement mounted as two or three teams contested the leadership of the league and rarely was the title won until the last afternoon of the season. No season, however, had a finale as dramatic or exciting as the year of 1976.

On the morning of the final Sunday of the season, 5 September, the position at the top of the league was as follows:

(1) Somerset 40 pts; (2) Sussex 40 pts; (3) Kent 36 pts; (4)
Essex 36 pts; (5) Leicestershire 36 pts.

Mathematically it was possible for each of these five teams to
win the league. Both Somerset and Sussex were playing away,
and if they were both victorious, they would be level on the
number of away wins as well as on points. In this event Somerset
would be winners of the league as they had a superior run rate
over the season. It is interesting to reflect that in the first year
of the John Player League the average number of runs per over
was 3.97, since when it has climbed steadily, with only
occasional hiccups, to 4.73 in 1981.

There was great excitement in the West Country as it was
felt, with justified confidence, that Somerset were on the verge
of winning the first honour in their one-hundred-and-one-year
history. Their last game was at Cardiff against Glamorgan,
bottom of the John Player League in 1975 and lying bottom of
the John Player League on the morning of Sunday, 5 September
1976. To Somerset supporters it mattered not what went on at
Edgbaston where Warwickshire were playing Sussex for they
believed that their side would be winners at Cardiff and so take
the League.

The BBC, anxious to be at the right spot for the presentation
of the trophy, had units at Edgbaston, Cardiff and Maidstone
where Kent were entertaining Gloucestershire. The trophy itself
was in Birmingham, but a helicopter was standing by to take it to
Cardiff or wherever else it should be needed. The helicopter was
to have something of a traumatic afternoon.

Very soon it became apparent that Kent would beat Gloucestershire. Woolmer and Tavare put on 75 for the first wicket in
eleven overs and then Asif Iqbal hit a hundred in eighty-two
minutes, including fifty off thirty-nine balls, the fastest televised
fifty of the season. Mike Denness also reached fifty and Kent's
278 for 5 had left Gloucestershire with the task of scoring 6.97
an over which, without Procter in the side, seemed a near impossibility. They began at four an over and then subsided
quietly. Kent would have to sit and wait to hear what had
happened elsewhere.

Essex beat Yorkshire by twelve runs at Leyton to remain
level on points with Kent and Leicestershire, who, with fewer
away wins, were victorious at The Oval.

At Edgbaston, Sussex's dreams of glory faded over by over. Rouse tore out their middle order and they could make only 149 in 38.5 overs. Waller retired hurt and was unable to bowl. Jameson started in characteristically violent mood and although Amiss and Whitehouse fell to Mike Buss and John Snow, Kanhai joined Jameson to hit off the runs at leisure.

This meant that Somerset needed only to tie their match at Cardiff to become John Player League champions.

One of the great ironies of the Somerset challenge was that it was being made under the leadership of Brian Close who had left Yorkshire six years earlier after some differences with the administration. One of those differences, it was reported, was Close's lack of concern for the limited-over game.

There were over seven thousand people at Cardiff to see the prospective champions meet the bottom-of-the-league side, but if Somerset supporters had believed that this would be an easy stroll to success, they were soon disabused. There was an edginess in the Somerset play, an over-striving that is always the failing of those on the threshold of untasted glory.

Alan Jones, one of the finest of cricketers and one whom the gods of cricket have not treated as kindly as they should have done when distributing honours, and Geoff Ellis started steadily. With the score at 31 Ellis was caught behind off Botham and Somerset breathed more easily.

Eight runs later, with his own score at 21, Alan Jones was missed by Brian Close. It was a cruel, but vital miss by the Somerset captain, a great fielder. Somerset had to wait until another 83 runs had been scored before they captured another wicket; more devastatingly, Jones went on to score 70, easily the highest score of the game.

In the thirty-nine overs that were bowled before ten past four, Glamorgan moved at even pace to 191.

What Somerset needed was a solid start against Nash and Cordle, who were by far the best and most successful of the Glamorgan bowlers that season. That good start did not come. With the score at 11, Peter Denning, a busy and eager cricketer, was lbw to Malcolm Nash. Four runs later Brian Close also fell to Nash.

The next man in was Ian Botham, not yet twenty-one years old and capped for Somerset earlier that season. He was to

make his Test debut the following year, but already he was
being recognised as a brilliant all-rounder of great power and
aggression. He smote a couple of mighty blows and then gave
Nash a return catch and Somerset were 27 for 3. The BBC
helicopter started its journey to Maidstone.

The priority for Rose and Kitchen was the reparation of the
Somerset innings. They played purposefully and added 70
before Rose was caught behind off Lawrence Williams. Kitchen
and Burgess maintained the Somerset challenge. With eight
overs remaining Somerset were 128 for 5, Kitchen having just
fallen to Wilkins.

In the next four overs Burgess and Dennis Breakwell, a spin
bowler and fierce hitter who had joined Somerset from Northants
in 1973, but had been capped only a few months before this
match, added 33 runs and a Somerset victory and the championship of the John Player League were within reach.

The dangerous Breakwell was bowled by Nash in the thirty-
seventh over. Somerset needed 18 from two overs. Taylor was
run out in the scamper for runs. Ten needed from the last over.

Jennings was run out in another dash for runs and the last
ball of the season arrived with Burgess needing to hit Nash for
four to win the match. A three will give Somerset a tie and the
two points they need to win the John Player League.

Burgess drove mightily at Nash, who had bowled splendidly,
and hit the ball high back over the bowler's head. Alan Jones,
whose 70 out of 134 had been the bane of Somerset earlier in
the day, now committed his final act of blight on their hopes.
He cut off the ball before it could reach the boundary and
threw fast and true to Nash. Burgess made his ground for the
third, vital run, but Dredge was not so quick. Nash threw to
Eifion Jones who whipped off the bails to leave Dredge still
inches short of making his ground.

Glamorgan had won by one run and Somerset were still
without a trophy after one hundred and one years of endeavour.
It was a bitter moment for them. Burgess stood, shoulders
drooped, in a mood of utter dejection. At a time of such
despair it seems that a chance of glory will never come again.

The BBC helicopter had gone to the right place after all and
the champagne flowed in the Kent dressing-room.

In fact, five teams had finished the season on forty points.

Kent and Essex both had five away wins. Kent's run rate was 4.988 to the 4.560 of Essex who, for the second time, had lost the John Player League by a narrow mathematical margin. But it was Somerset for whom most sympathy was felt and for the brave Graham Burgess in particular.

GLAMORGAN *v* SOMERSET
John Player League
at Cardiff
5 September 1976

Glamorgan

A. Jones (capt)	b Dredge	70
G.P. Ellis	c Taylor, b Botham	12
D.A. Francis	b Jennings	36
M.A. Nash	b Moseley	43
J.A. Hopkins	run out	7
A.E. Cordle	c Rose, b Botham	9
* E.W. Jones	run out	0
G. Richards	not out	0
A.H. Wilkins		
B.J. Lloyd		
D.L. Williams		
Extras	b 12, lb 1, nb 1	14
	(for 7 wkts)	191

	O	M	R	W
Moseley	8	—	31	1
Botham	7	—	41	2
Burgess	8	—	32	—
Jennings	8	—	39	1
Dredge	8	—	34	1

fall of wickets
1–31, 2–123, 3–134, 4–145, 5–180, 6–189, 7–190

Somerset

B.C. Rose	c E.W. Jones, b Williams	39
P.W. Denning	lbw, b Nash	6
D.B. Close (capt)	c Wilkins, b Nash	1
I.T. Botham	c and b Nash	9
M.J. Kitchen	b Wilkins	46
G.I. Burgess	not out	48
D. Breakwell	b Nash	21
• D.J.S. Taylor	run out	8
K.F. Jennings	run out	1
C.H. Dredge	run out	0
H.R. Moseley		
Extras	lb 10, nb 1	11
	(for 9 wkts)	190

	O	M	R	W
Nash	8	1	35	4
Cordle	8	1	38	—
Ellis	8	—	34	—
Lloyd	4	—	17	—
Williams	7	—	32	1
Wilkins	4	—	23	1

fall of wickets
1—11, 2—15, 3—27, 4—97, 5—127, 6—171, 7—180, 8—188, 9—190

Glamorgan won by 1 run

HAMPSHIRE v GLOUCESTERSHIRE

BENSON AND HEDGES CUP SEMI-FINAL

At Southampton

22 June 1977

In 1963, the South African schools' side which toured England included two young men who were later to make a devastating impact on the world of cricket. One was the captain of the side, Barry Anderson Richards; and the other was the vice-captain, Michael John Procter.

Barry Richards was to become recognised as one of the very greatest batsmen that the game has known. Because the politics of his country has isolated them from the rest of the world, his Test career was all too brief. In 1969–70, he played in the last series that South Africa played before being excommunicated and in the four Tests against Australia he scored 508 runs at an average of 72.57.

Perhaps soured by finding himself like an Alexander without even the prospect of a world to conquer, he became something of a cricketing mercenary, playing most of his cricket in Australia and England.

After a flirtation with Gloucestershire he joined Hampshire in 1968 and for ten years he adorned the county scene as he and Gordon Greenidge formed one of the most memorable, and certainly the most exciting, opening partnership of all time. But he tired of the seven-day-a-week county circuit and left Hampshire abruptly in 1978. There was a feeling of regret that he had not chosen to apply himself more often. When he was in the mood, or the occasion was right, particularly when there was a large crowd and the television cameras were present, he displayed a talent that few have ever approached and to see him in full flow was the greatest of glories. There were other days when it seemed that he simply could not be bothered and there was a sense of wasted genius.

For more than a decade Mike Procter was Gloucestershire. He brought back fire and interest to an ailing county, and there was excitement in the air. He bowled at a fearsome pace, albeit off the wrong foot, and he smote the ball harder and higher than any since Jessop. He also bowled off-breaks and fielded splendidly, as did Richards, so that no captain could ever feel himself immune from defeat when Procter was in the other side.

He captained with enthusiasm and led by example. He revelled in World Series Cricket for it gave him the opportunity to contend at international level, a chance that had been denied him, like Richards, since 1970. His seven Test matches brought him 226 runs and forty-one wickets at a very low cost. In 1970–71 he scored six centuries in successive innings in South Africa and one can only ponder on what he would have achieved at Test level had the world been saner.

With Richards in the side Hampshire won the County Championship in 1973 and the John Player League in 1975. With Procter, Gloucestershire had won the Gillette Cup in 1973, their first honour since the days of W.G. Grace, and were consistently pressing for titles in the mid-seventies.

For all their success at the limited-over game Hampshire had failed to reach either of the knock-out finals. They had been defeated semi-finalists in the Gillette Cup of 1966 and 1976 and they had lost in the semi-final of the Benson and Hedges Cup in 1975.

1977 saw Hampshire and Gloucestershire drawn together in the same qualifying group. Gloucestershire beat Somerset in the opening match, and then Hampshire overwhelmed Gloucestershire at Bristol.

Gloucestershire made 201 for 9 in their fifty-five overs and Hampshire got the runs for the loss of only two wickets with more than *seventeen* overs to spare. Greenidge hit a hundred. They then beat Lancashire, but lost to Somerset. Victory over Leicestershire assured them of a place in the quarter-finals and as Gloucestershire won their remaining matches they too were in the last eight.

Hampshire pulverised Glamorgan at Swansea while Gloucestershire had a narrow win over Middlesex. There was now excitement that these two sides would meet in the final and that Lord's would be the scene of a mighty contest between Richards, who had scored few runs in the tournament so far, and Procter.

The draw deemed otherwise and Southampton in the semi-final was the meeting place of the giants.

It was a day of high summer. The ground was full. The best of the seating had been captured early and now there was a jostle for vantage places even if it meant standing.

Andy Stovold and Sadiq Mohammad came out to open the Gloucestershire innings and there was evidence of much support for the visitors. The Gloucestershire support was always a noisy one.

The first few overs are vital. In a Test match, a county match or a limited-over game, the opening overs can so often shape the course of what is to come. Hampshire's strength was not in their bowling. Derek Shackleton, Peter Sainsbury, Bob Cottam and 'Butch' White had all gone and their successors were containers rather than attackers. There was the nagging accuracy of the ever-reliable Mike Taylor and the equally persistent medium pace of Trevor Jesty, but Mottram, Rice and Murtagh were of less dependable quality. Much rested on Andy Roberts, but his appetite for the county game had dulled, and, in fact, in 1977, Rice and Mottram were more successful bowlers than Roberts in the limited-over game. Nevertheless, he remained the bowler that Gloucestershire most feared and the one that had to be countered.

Stovold and Sadiq allayed their supporters' apprehensions with a most solid start. Roberts was denied his break-through and the batsmen settled down to prosper. And prosper they did.

Sadiq was in splendid form, cutting and pulling in that violently chunky manner which made him such a bubbling delight to watch when he was in his prime.

Stovold was less adventurous, more limited, but he is an effective player. He plays correctly, never perhaps asserting his personality, but he gathers runs quickly and quietly and there was a time when one believed that he would play for England.

The wicket was easy. The undulating outfield at Southampton is usually quick and it is never the easiest of grounds on which to field. Runs flowed and with Zaheer Abbas, Mike Procter and the fine hitting of the burly David Shepherd to come, Gloucestershire were moving into a position of ascendancy.

Sadiq and Stovold put on 106 for the first wicket before Stovold fell to Mottram. It was a fine start and one which

seemed to assure a big total for Gloucestershire, but they
faltered. With the stage set for them Zaheer and Procter forgot
their lines. Sadiq's aggressive innings came to an end. Shepherd
was run out in the late scramble as seven wickets went down for
18 runs and, incredibly, Gloucestershire were all out for 180
with four balls of their quota unused.

Hampshire supporters were almost as stunned by the collapse
as their rivals, but they were now totally convinced that the
home side would stroll to victory on their own ground. Since
lunch there had been a dramatic change in the fortunes of the
two sides, but the drama had only just begun.

Procter and Brain opened the Gloucestershire bowling.
Procter gave early indication that he would work up to his full
pace, but Richards and Greenidge began crisply enough. They
negotiated two overs from Procter and two from Brain and
Hampshire's confidence grew.

It was Procter's third over which dispelled all complacency.
His fifth ball beat Greenidge and knocked the stumps askew.
13 for 1. Turner survived the last ball of the over.

Brain's third over produced 5 runs, Richards was as yet
circumspect.

He shaped to receive the first ball of Procter's fourth over.
His bat was raised in that characteristic accentuated back-lift.
Richards' greatness as a batsman was founded upon the quick-
ness with which he could pick up line and length and therefore
the rapidity with which he positioned himself for the correct
shot. This time he was beaten by Procter's pace. The ball hit
him on the pad. There was a raucous appeal and Tom Spencer's
finger went up. There was gloom in Hampshire.

Greater gloom was to follow. Trevor Jesty took guard. He
was beaten for pace by Procter's first ball to him. He was struck
on the pad. Again there was an appeal. Again umpire Spencer's
finger went up.

Next was John Rice. He was beaten completely by Procter's
first ball to him and the stumps were spreadeagled. The Gloucestershire captain had taken four wickets in five balls, all of
them front-line batsmen. He had done the hat-trick and Hampshire were in ruins at 18 for 4.

It was one of the greatest, if not the greatest bowling performance ever accomplished in limited-over cricket, not only in

the class of batsmen that had been dismissed, but also in the importance of the occasion, the intensity of the struggle.

Hampshire supporters were astounded. In the space of three minutes the dreams of victory had been shattered. There was no hope remaining.

At the wicket now were Nigel Cowley, a twenty-four-year-old all-rounder whose off-breaks were rarely used in the one-day game, and the left-hander David Turner.

Turner is a player of immense class. He first played for Wiltshire before making his debut for Hampshire in 1966. He was recognised immediately as a player of quality and there were confident predictions that he would play for England. Against Lillee and the 1972 Australians he had hit a hundred for Hampshire at Southampton and the tourists rated him as one of the very best batsmen that they encountered on the tour, but he suffered an eye injury later that summer. Then, against the 1975 Australians he scored 87 in the first innings, but he had a finger broken by Jeff Thomson in the second and somehow the injuries have prevented him from becoming quite the player one had expected. There are still many less competent and attractive players who have represented England while Turner has been making his runs for Hampshire.

Cowley and Turner were Hampshire's last hope of a miracle for there was little to come after them. This was not time for the flashing blade. The first consideration must be for survival and to withstand what remained of Procter and Brain in their opening spell.

The first task was accomplished and against the lesser demands of Shackleton, Partridge, Graveney and Vernon they began to push along the score. The fifty was reached and they edged the score closer to the hundred. Hampshire supporters dared to believe that they were witnessing the start of the miracle for which they had prayed.

They added 109 of the bravest runs and the partnership was only ended when Procter deemed that Brain must be brought back into the attack before this stand got completely out of hand. The ploy worked for Brain bowled Turner when the left-hander was one short of his fifty.

At the very end of his spell Shackleton did the greatest damage against his father's old county when he bowled Cowley

for 59. It remains his highest score in the Benson and Hedges
Cup competition and it is an innings of which he remains
justifiably proud.

Now Hampshire fell apart again. Turner and Cowley had
added 109 for the fifth wicket, but the overs were running out
and as the batsmen pressed for runs five wickets fell for 32 runs.
They were left with Tom Mottram, highest score 15 not out,
who had played only in one-day matches and was soon to leave
the game entirely, and Andy Roberts.

Roberts can hit a ball very hard, as even Test bowlers have
found, and he played his natural game. Mottram got his bat in
the way and still Hampshire breathed hope. With four balls
remaining eight runs were needed to win and Brian Brain was
bowling.

In a bid for death or glory Roberts swung his bat. It was
death. The ball was straight and he missed. Gloucestershire had
won by seven runs.

Mike Procter's final figures were 6 for 13, the most decisive
match-winning bowling that the Benson and Hedges tournament
has ever seen. It was no surprise that he took the gold award,
but there were congratulations too for Sadiq and Stovold, for
Mike Taylor who had bowled Hampshire back into the game,
for the wily Brain, and especially for the courageous Turner and
Cowley who had refused to admit defeat when most had given
up hope after those four terrifying deliveries by Mike Procter.

HAMPSHIRE *v* GLOUCESTERSHIRE
Benson and Hedges Cup Semi-Final
at Southampton
22 June 1977

Gloucestershire

* A.W. Stovold	c Turner, b Mottram	46
Sadiq Mohammad	c Greenidge, b Rice	76
Zaheer Abbas	c Richards, b Jesty	11
M.J. Procter (capt)	c Greenidge, b Taylor	8
D.R. Shepherd	run out	18
J.C. Foat	c Stephenson, b Taylor	1
M.D. Partridge	b Taylor	0
D.A. Graveney	not out	5
J.H. Shackleton	st Stephenson, b Mottram	1
M.J. Vernon	c Jesty, b Mottram	2
B.M. Brain	b Roberts	2
Extras	b 1, lb 8, nb 1	10
		180

	O	M	R	W
Roberts	10.2	3	20	1
Mottram	10	2	21	3
Taylor	11	1	37	3
Rice	11	—	39	1
Jesty	11	1	39	1
Murtagh	1	—	14	—

fall of wickets
1—106, 2—121, 3—146, 4—162, 5—164, 6—168, 7—169, 8—174, 9—176

Hampshire

B.A. Richards	lbw, b Procter	3
C.G. Greenidge	b Procter	9
D.R. Turner	b Brain	49
T.E. Jesty	lbw, b Procter	0
J.M. Rice	b Procter	0
N.G. Cowley	b Shackleton	59
M.N.S. Taylor	c Stovold, b Procter	4
A.J. Murtagh	c Stovold, b Brain	1
* G.R. Stephenson (capt)	b Procter	10
A.M.E. Roberts	b Brain	17
T.J. Mottram	not out	3
Extras	lb 9, nb 9	18
		173

	O	M	R	W
Procter	11	5	13	6
Brain	10.3	4	28	3
Shackleton	11	4	33	1
Partridge	6	1	22	—
Graveney	6	—	24	—
Vernon	10	2	35	—

fall of wickets
1—13, 2—18, 3—18, 4—18, 5—127, 6—137, 7—138, 8—144, 9—159

Gloucestershire won by 7 runs

MIDDLESEX v GLAMORGAN

GILLETTE CUP FINAL

At Lord's

3 September 1977

The Gillette Cup final of 1977 was not a great cricketing contest. There was no breathtaking finish and the side that was expected to win did win, and by five wickets with more than four overs to spare. Yet the match was a good one. It produced some absorbing cricket and it was played in fine spirit before a good-humoured crowd. There had been fears as to crowd behaviour following scenes at the Benson and Hedges Cup final earlier in the season, but the Middlesex and Glamorgan supporters were impeccably behaved and it was a delightful occasion.

The most remarkable thing was that the game took place at all. It had seemed to rain unceasingly throughout August. The semi-finals of the competition had been scheduled for 17 August, but the game at Swansea between Glamorgan and Lancashire had taken three days to complete. The match at Lord's between Somerset and Middlesex was finally decided on 26 August. The first three days were completely washed out so that the three-day County Championship match scheduled for 24, 25 and 26 August was postponed to allow the match to be played. Again no play was possible on the first two days and Middlesex reached the final when they beat Somerset in a fifteen-over game on the Friday morning. Somerset, in fact, were bowled out for 59 in 14.4 overs.

The final was only a week away when Glamorgan found out who their opponents were to be. The surprise to most people was that Glamorgan should be in the final themselves. They had won the County Championship in 1969 since when times had been hard. By 1977 only four of that championship side remained. They had never before reached the final of one of the limited-over competitions, and neither before, nor since, have they got as far as the semi-finals.

They had something of a resurgence in 1977, but they still

finished fourteenth in the championship table and their position
of eighth in the John Player League that season was the highest
position they have ever finished in that competition.

By contrast Middlesex were an emerging power in the land.
In 1975 they had reached the finals of the Gillette Cup and the
Benson and Hedges Cup. They were well beaten in both finals,
but they had given indication that Mike Brearley was shaping a
forceful team who would soon contend for all honours.

In 1976, Brearley's astute leadership saw them win the
County Championship and a year later, with Wayne Daniel in the
side, they shared the title with Kent. They also finished third in
the John Player League so that it was obvious that they would
come to Lord's as favourites to win the Gillette Cup.

Against such formidable opponents many would have wilted,
but Glamorgan were never short of spirit and although the
defeat was conclusive enough in the end, it may all have been
very different but for one dropped catch.

In the history of the Gillette Cup Mike Brearley became the
first captain to ask the opposition to bat when he won the toss
and to justify his decision with victory. On the day before the
game it had rained for hours in London and it was evening
before the clouds finally passed away. Once more it was the
marvellous work of Jim Fairbrother and his staff that made play
possible and the match started on time. It was probably the
dampness of the outfield, however, which prompted Brearley's
decision for it certainly cost Glamorgan some runs with its
slowness at the start.

Balancing this was the fact that the softness of the pitch
tended to nullify the threat of Wayne Daniel for it was he
whom Glamorgan had feared above all others. If Daniel was less
of a threat, the same could not be said of Mike Selvey who
bowled an accurate length and moved the ball disconcertingly
from the very start.

Alan Jones, who had just completed a thousand runs in a first-
class season for the seventeenth year in succession, opened the
innings with John Hopkins who was enjoying a splendid season.

Mention is made elsewhere in this volume of the qualities of
Alan Jones. Here is one of the great professionals and here he
was leading his side in one of the very great days in their history.
He is a man conscious of history and of position. If he erred this

day, it was in that he pressed for runs right from the start. In an
endeavour to get his side off to a brisk start he tried too much
too soon. He had scored all but three of the first twenty-one
runs when he attempted to hit a little adventurously against the
persistent Selvey and was lbw.

Hopkins was playing with the good sense expected of one
who had recently been awarded his county cap, and he played
some crisp shots that did not always bring the runs they deserved.
He was now partnered by Collis King and here was Glamorgan's
first big disappointment of the match.

Those who saw King in the Prudential World Cup final of
1979 will never forget the brilliance of his batting and there are
those who contend that he was one of the outstanding successes
of World Series Cricket. For Glamorgan, he flitted briefly and few
were surprised to see him depart. There were days when he
struck some lusty blows, but they were few and far between,
and the days were fewer when his bowling was anything more
than mediocre. But always with players of such power and
potential there are hopes that this could be the day and when
he gathered a few runs and the score crept into the forties,
Welsh fans dared to suspect that he had chosen the final to
reveal his true glory. He had not. He hit to cover where Barlow
caught him comfortably to give Selvey his second wicket.

There was a further disappointment for Glamorgan three runs
later when Rodney Ontong, a week short of his twenty-second
birthday and a young man of aggression and immense promise,
a promise which, perhaps, has never been fully realised, was
caught behind off Mike Gatting who was used as Middlesex's
third seamer. This meant that Glamorgan had lost their three
leading batsmen for fifty runs and those who had predicted a
one-sided final were being proved right.

The next man in was Mike Llewellyn, a tall left-hander, who,
though not yet twenty-four, had first played for Glamorgan
seven years earlier. He had been capped only that season when
his sole century had been made against Oxford University, 129
not out, which has remained a career best.

Mike Llewellyn has rarely held a regular place in the Glamorgan
side since 1977. The fire, the passion, the courage, the potential
are still apparent, but the years are passing. In 1981, in nine
first-class innings he averaged only 5.37. He played in only three

limited-over games during the season. But whatever has happened since, however bitter the disappointments, few will ever forget his innings in Glamorgan's only appearance in the Gillette Cup final.

He began with 4, 6, 4 off Gatting as his first scoring strokes. Momentarily, he and Hopkins revived Glamorgan's hopes as they added 65 before Hopkins was bowled by Phil Edmonds.

The Middlesex bowling was tight and the fielding superb. Brearley, relishing the intellectual challenge that the game presented, was always in complete command. His bowling changes were tactical, never merely mathematical. He exerted benevolent authority and his team responded unswervingly. Gordon Ross selected Mike Gatting as the outstanding fielder to receive the Learie Constantine Award donated by the Wombwell Cricket Lovers' Society, but as he admitted later, he could have chosen half a dozen others without complaint, and few would have argued if he had selected Brearley.

The boldness of Llewellyn remained Glamorgan's one hope of reaching a substantial score. John Emburey was bowling with economy when Llewellyn hit him for the most memorable shot that was ever played in a Gillette Cup final. He drove Emburey straight to the pavilion, a hit so colossal that the ball landed in the guttering near the BBC commentary box at the top of the pavilion. It was a huge and courageous achievement and when all else is forgotten of this final it will be remembered. One can only think of Keith Miller in the years since the war who has made a hit of comparable size.

The brave knock of Mike Llewellyn ended when he lofted Norman Featherstone, whose off-spin Brearley had pressed into service to great effect, to Mike Gatting. He had scored 62 thrilling runs and it remains his highest score in the Gillette Cup.

Glamorgan had little else to offer and the total of 177 for 9 seemingly posed few problems for Middlesex.

The sun was now shining. The sky was blue and all seemed well when Brearley and Smith set out on the road to victory for Middlesex.

Malcolm Nash opened the bowling for Glamorgan. Left-arm over, with brisk late movement, his first ball swung away from Brearley's forward shot and Eifion Jones threw the ball in the air gleefully. 0 for 1 off one ball and there was a chance that Glamorgan could still surprise people.

The Middlesex score reached four. It was Nash's second over. Malcolm Nash is a cricketer and a man of the greatest heart. He lives and breathes Glamorgan and he believes that every boy in the county should nurse in his heart the desire to play for the county, and that the county should be worthy of those young ambitions. He had tasted blood. He was bowling with fire. He believed that Glamorgan could, and would, win. He swung the ball late away from Radley's probing bat. The batsman was left helpless as the ball clipped the edge and went straight to Collis King at second slip for the simplest of catches. The West Indian dropped it. Radley had scored two at the time.

Now Radley assumed authority. As he prospered so Glamorgan faded. Chances and half-chances went begging. Mike Smith gave Radley solid support and when he was dismissed there was Gatting to hold an end. Barlow was brisk and efficient and there was a restlessness and inevitability about the batting which affected Glamorgan. The match ebbed away and they died quietly with Clive Radley's innings flowering to a Man-of-the-Match performance in his benefit year.

The prophets had been proved right. Middlesex had won easily and Brearley waved the cup on high. It was not a great final and yet it had given one man the chance to play what proved to be the innings of his life. He had also hit one of the most memorable shots ever seen at Lord's and another man had missed a slip catch which cost his side dear and for which, in the valleys, he was never forgiven.

MIDDLESEX *v* GLAMORGAN
Gillette Cup Final
at Lord's
3 September 1977

Glamorgan

A. Jones (capt)	lbw, b Selvey	18
J.A. Hopkins	b Edmonds	47
C.L. King	c Barlow, b Selvey	8
R.C. Ontong	c Gould, b Gatting	0
M.J. Llewellyn	c Gatting, b Featherstone	62
G. Richards	b Edmonds	3
* E.W. Jones	run out	11
M.A. Nash	c Gatting, b Featherstone	3
A.E. Cordle	not out	8
T.W. Cartwright	st Gould, b Featherstone	3
A.H. Wilkins		
Extras	b 7, lb 5, w 2	14
	(for 9 wkts)	177

	O	M	R	W
Daniel	11	—	41	—
Selvey	12	4	22	2
Gatting	7	1	28	1
Edmonds	12	3	23	2
Emburey	12	2	32	—
Featherstone	6	—	17	3

fall of wickets
1—21, 2—47, 3—50, 4—115, 5—129, 6—163, 7—163, 8—171, 9—177

Middlesex

J.M. Brearley (capt)	c E.W. Jones, b Nash	0
M.J. Smith	lbw, b Cartwright	22
C.T. Radley	not out	85
M.W. Gatting	c Hopkins, b King	15
G.D. Barlow	lbw, b Richards	27
N.G. Featherstone	b Nash	3
P.H. Edmonds	not out	9
* I.J. Gould		
J.E. Emburey		
M.W.W. Selvey		
W.W. Daniel		
Extras	b 6, lb 11	17
	(for 5 wkts)	178

	O	M	R	W
Nash	12	3	31	2
Cordle	8.4	1	29	—
Cartwright	12	2	32	1
King	5	1	19	1
Richards	12	2	23	1
Wilkins	6	—	27	—

fall of wickets
1—0, 2—45, 3—72, 4—146, 5—153

Middlesex won by 5 wickets

SOMERSET v ESSEX

GILLETTE CUP SEMI-FINAL

At Taunton

16 August 1978

By the late seventies, Essex and Somerset alone of the seventeen first-class counties had not won a major trophy, yet they were two of the strongest sides in the country.

In 1978, it appeared that both sides had reached their peak. Essex challenged Kent for the Schweppes County Championship to the very last. Somerset were deprived of the John Player League when they lost to Essex in the last game of the season. They had also reached the semi-final of the Benson and Hedges Cup where they were beaten by Kent.

There was growing excitement as the Gillette Cup progressed and Essex and Somerset proved successful that these two would be contesting the final, but the draw brought them together in the semi-final at Taunton. It was heralded as the match of the season. For many it turned out to be the match of the century.

Taunton is not a large ground and although it has been developed in recent years to keep pace with Somerset's success, for the semi-final of the 1978 Gillette Cup it was bursting at the seams with supporters of both teams. Indeed the ground was uncomfortably full. There is a fierce rivalry between these two sides. Between their supporters it is mostly friendly, at least until the cider and the Adnams take over.

The atmosphere was tense, the crowd noisy, when the captains came out to toss up. The wicket was slightly damp and likely to give some assistance to the bowlers in the early stages, so Rose, on winning the toss, was confronted with a difficult decision. In Richards and Botham he had batsmen who were good at chasing a target. In Garner and Botham he had bowlers who were fine at exploiting advantageous conditions. Against these considerations was the fact that he had put Kent in to bat in the semi-final of the Benson and Hedges Cup and it had cost him the match. After some hesitation he decided that Somerset would bat first and Essex took the field.

Rose's fears were confirmed when Slocombe was lbw to Norbert Phillip in the second over of the innings. First blow to Essex. Next man in, Viv Richards. The second ball that Richards received from Phillip was despatched to the mid-wicket boundary. Somerset supporters breathed more easily. The hero was in form.

They were less certain of this fact in Phillip's next over when Richards was twice beaten outside the off-stump. Lever was bowling well and swinging the ball appreciably. He found the outside edge of Richards' bat when the West Indian was on twenty-two, but to the chagrin of all Essex the catch was put down at first slip. Worse was to follow when, in Lever's next over, Rose was also dropped at slip. These missed chances were in sharp contrast to the rest of the Essex fielding which was of the very highest quality.

The Rose—Richards stand began to prosper. The pitch had given some help to the seamers, but it was now drying out to placidity. Essex had lost their advantage with those two dropped catches. You cannot give Viv Richards a second chance without paying the price.

Stuart Turner came on to bowl a succession of maidens at Rose. It was a combination of relentlessly accurate bowling by a fierce competitor and solid defence by a batsman determined that his side would succeed. He maintained his place at the wicket while Richards sprayed the field with his shots.

Ironically, it was not Turner who took Rose's wicket but Pont. 86 for 2 and Essex still had a chance to contain Somerset. Richards thought otherwise.

Roebuck was becalmed at first, but it mattered little. Richards was now in full flow, dissecting the field with awesome power. Three times he lofted Pont to the boundary so that Fletcher was forced to withdraw him from the attack. When the economical Turner returned he, too, was savaged. Richards hit him off both the front and back foot with such force that fielders could only stand in amazement as the ball sped to the boundary. East was driven for six over extra cover. Richards had once more become a giant among men and the mere mortals could do nothing but gaze in wonder.

In all he batted for forty-five overs and he hit a five and fourteen fours as well as the six off East. It took a superb catch at mid-wicket by Mike Denness to end his innings. 116 out of 189 for 3.

It was imperative that Somerset should not lose the impetus that had been given them by Richards' marvellous innings, and Peter Roebuck, who batted with intelligence for thirty overs, now took on responsibility and accelerated. Botham failed, but Vic Marks hit cleanly from the start. When Roebuck was well caught Breakwell joined Marks in some ferocious batting, Burgess having fallen to Lever.

The last ten overs of the innings added a vital 79 runs and for once the Essex bowling and the Essex captain erred. The usually reliable Lever was punished mercilessly and many felt that Turner, who had conceded runs in only two overs, and those to Richards, should have been brought back to complete his quota.

Essex faced a formidable task even though the wicket was easy, the outfield fast and the ground a small one. Much depended on a sound opening and on whether or not Gooch or McEwan could play a substantial innings.

The sound opening did not come. Denness was caught off Dredge at 9. Garner, of course, was always dangerous, being able to extract unexpected lift from his great height. Dredge, the honest county bowler, has a nip and a movement that has won him the description of 'The Terror of Frome' from Alan Gibson.

It was these two whom Gooch and McEwan first had to counter. Gooch was dropped when 15, but he and his South African partner were scoring at the necessary rate. They had taken the score to 70 and seen off the opening attack when McEwan, over ambitious, swung at the moderate medium pace of Burgess and was bowled.

Fletcher had a most unhappy start and was constantly beaten by Botham, but he survived. He and Gooch had taken the score to 106 off twenty-four overs just before tea when Rose called up Marks for the last over before the interval. Without any risk the batsmen took 13 runs from the over to put Essex exactly on course for victory.

Gooch was caught behind off Garner at 127 and now came the key stand of the match. Hardie and Fletcher added 39, but the overs slipped away, and they were being bowled at this stage by the least of the Somerset bowlers. Hardie was run out by

Slocombe in the forty-second over when Essex needed 122 for victory. Nearly seven runs an over against Garner, Botham and Dredge was asking much, but Keith Pont gave a hint that victory was possible when he hit Richards for six. Fletcher now at last began to time the ball and these two added 80 runs at over six an over.

Forty-two were needed from five overs when Botham ran out Pont from third man and caught and bowled Fletcher in successive overs. Phillip was run out in the skelter for runs and Turner hit Botham for two incredibly grotesque and unorthodox fours before the gods ceased to smile on him.

So we reached the last over. Smith and East at the wicket. Dredge bowling. Twelve runs required for an Essex victory for Essex had already lost more wickets than Somerset.

Dredge bowls to Smith who pushes forward for a single. Eleven needed off five balls. Dredge moves in again and East lunges. The ball shoots off the edge and beats the despairing dive of third man to cross the boundary for four. The Essex supporters shout hysterically as they realise that seven runs in four balls is within the realms of possibility even with every Somerset player bar wicket-keeper and bowler ringing the boundary. Their hysteria is quietened when Dredge bowls the next ball. East swings and the stumps are scattered.

John Lever walks to the wicket with Somerset supporters chanting in anticipation of victory. As he takes guard the noise subsides. Numbers nine, ten and eleven are the most unenviable positions in the side. They rarely bat and when they do they are asked either to score quick runs or to save the side. As a number eleven Lever is a batsman of better quality than most. Three balls to go, seven needed.

The fourth ball of the over produces the totally unexpected. There is a cry of elation from Essex and total dismay from Somerset as Colin Dredge, striving for that grain of extra pace in the tension of the moment, bowls a no-ball. Lever pushes it for a single and Somerset reveal a corporate nervousness when, in a flurry of excitement and panic, the ball is thrown wildly for two overthrows. Four runs are needed from three balls and Essex supporters regain their voices.

Dredge to Smith. A violent swing and there is no contact. Cheers and chants echo round the ground from the Somerset supporters. Smith nudges a single off the sixth ball of the over and so we reach the last ball of the match with Essex needing three runs for victory and Somerset needing only to prevent them from scoring them.

There is a constant roar as Dredge moves in to bowl to Lever. The batsman swings the ball round to fine-leg where Rose is running in from the boundary. Smith hurtles down the wicket and they cross for one. Rose fails to gather the ball as he runs in and the batsmen have crossed for the second run.

Rose picks up and throws to Taylor. Smith, summoning speed which few thought he possessed, is striving for the line. He dives and there is a flurry of dust, batsman, wicket-keeper and falling bails. Somerset throw their arms in the air in appeal. The umpire's finger is raised and Somerset have won — by an inch.

In all, 574 runs have been scored in the day at a rate of 4.78 an over. And in the end the scores have finished level.

SOMERSET *v* ESSEX
Gillette Cup Semi-Final
at Taunton
16 August 1978

Somerset

B.C. Rose (capt)	c East, b Pont	24
P.A. Slocombe	lbw, b Phillip	0
I.V.A. Richards	c Denness, b Gooch	116
P.M. Roebuck	c Lever, b Phillip	57
I.T. Botham	b East	7
V.J. Marks	not out	33
G.I. Burgess	b Lever	5
D. Breakwell	not out	17
• D.J.S. Taylor		
J. Garner		
C.H. Dredge		
Extras	b 10, lb 14, w 1, nb 3	28
	(for 6 wkts)	287

	O	M	R	W
Lever	12	–	61	1
Phillip	11	1	56	2
Turner	8	6	22	–
Pont	6	1	35	1
Gooch	12	–	42	1
East	11	1	43	1

fall of wickets
1–2, 2–86, 3–189, 4–208, 5–247, 6–255

Essex

M.H. Denness	c Marks, b Dredge	3
G.A. Gooch	c Taylor, b Garner	61
K.S. McEwan	b Burgess	37
K.W.R. Fletcher (capt)	c and b Botham	67
B.R. Hardie	run out	21
K.R. Pont	run out	39
N. Phillip	run out	1
S. Turner	b Botham	12
R.E. East	b Dredge	10
N. Smith	run out	6
J.K. Lever	not out	5
Extras	b 14, lb 9, nb 2	25
		287

	O	M	R	W
Garner	12	1	46	1
Dredge	12	—	60	2
Botham	12	1	48	2
Burgess	12	1	43	1
Breakwell	2	—	11	—
Marks	1	—	13	—
Richards	9	1	41	—

fall of wickets
1—9, 2—70, 3—127, 4—166, 5—246, 6—248, 7—248, 8—266, 9—281

Somerset won on losing fewer wickets with scores level

ENGLAND v WEST INDIES

PRUDENTIAL WORLD CUP FINAL

At Lord's

23 June 1979

The second Prudential World Cup was preluded by the 'Packer Affair'. Its effect upon the competition in the end became minimal; the West Indies, under domestic pressure, included their World Series players, as did Pakistan who had been mutilated by England the previous summer when they played a series without their star players. The one country to remain devastated by the defection to Mr Packer's organisation was Australia whose side was bereft of some six or seven players who would have been first choices. It was not a happy time for the Australians.

By contrast England were in buoyant mood. Knott, Woolmer, Underwood and Greig had gone, but Brearley's side had had much success and there was a belief that they could snatch the world title from the West Indians.

Initially the weather was most unkind. The new ICC Trophy, the competition for the associate members, suffered badly as the picturesque club grounds of the Midlands, for which many matches had been scheduled, became awash. Sri Lanka, predictably, and Canada, surprisingly, qualified for the main competition and the weather improved.

England disposed of Australia with ease, and they beat Canada in the dark and the drizzle. The vital match was the one with Pakistan at Headingley. England recovered from 4 for 2 to reach 165 for 9, a total which looked inadequate until Mike Hendrick, in an inspired spell, reduced Pakistan to 34 for 6. They recovered through Asif Iqbal and Wasim Raja, but, in the end, it was two wickets by Geoff Boycott which gave England a narrow victory.

Pakistan still found a place in the semi-finals where they lost a splendid game to the West Indies who had been easy winners of their group in which New Zealand had finished second and Sri Lanka, who scored an historic win over India, third.

The semi-final between England and New Zealand produced some fine cricket and England did not claim victory until the penultimate ball of the match. The New Zealanders came very close to winning a place in the final, which their enthusiasm and application seemed to deserve.

The weather for the day of the final was as glorious as the occasion. Hosts v Holders and Lord's in all its glory.

The first problem for England was in selection. Their original choice of fourteen had not been wise. John Lever, in the middle of his *annus mirabilis*, was omitted and Mike Gatting, then far from international standard, was included. In the event Gatting did not play in a single game and when Willis was declared unfit for the final the paucity of the original selection became apparent. There was no obvious replacement for him. Edmonds was brought back into the side in place of Miller. This meant that England's fifth bowler had to be Boycott, or a combination of Gooch, Boycott and Larkins. Larkins had been another controversial selection. He had been chosen as an all-rounder, but at the time of his selection he had bowled only three overs in first-class cricket in the season and in the limited-over game he had sent down seventeen overs which had yielded 2 for 85. He was still some months away from his unhappy introduction to Test cricket. The 'fifth bowler' was thought to be, and proved to be, England's Achilles heel.

With the West Indian supporters already beginning their rhythmic accompaniment to the day's entertainment, Brearley won the toss and asked the champions to bat. Whatever his reasoning, the first England success had nothing to do with it.

Along with Gooch, Gordon Greenidge had been the outstanding batsman of the competition. He was a player whom England feared for he could tear an attack apart in very quick time. It was he who opened the innings with the quieter Desmond Haynes, still something of an unknown talent to the English public.

The sun was shining; the crowd was bubbling with excitement. The batsmen began quietly. Maiden overs by Hendrick and Botham were greeted with ecstasies of patriotic applause.

The score moved uneventfully to 22 before Greenidge played a ball to mid-wicket and went for the run. Randall's under-arm throw hit the stumps before Greenidge could make his ground

and England were jubilant at the removal of this potential
scourge.

The great Viv Richards was most uncertain at the start,
particularly against Edmonds, but he survived. Haynes did not.
An outswinger from Old had him caught at second slip by
Hendrick who cupped the ball with ease.

Kallicharran was the next man in. He had not enjoyed a good
season and there was to be no revival now. With astute captaincy,
Brearley brought Hendrick back into the attack and he clipped
Kallicharran's leg-stump. 55 for 3.

Clive Lloyd meandered from the pavilion for what would
surely be the crucial partnership of the match. If this partnership were broken, it was thought, then England were on the
edge of triumph.

The West Indies captain started circumspectly, but then he
began to strike the ball more firmly. The stand threatened
England ominously. Old was bowling from the pavilion end and
Lloyd drove the ball hard. Stooping to his left, Old held the ball
close to the ground. The West Indies were 99 for 4 and England
were winning.

Collis King was next and England had no great fear of him.
He had seemed a moderate cricketer, greatly vulnerable, in his
days with Glamorgan. But he was quickly into his stride. At
lunch he was still there and so was Viv Richards with a fifty to
his name of which, initially, he had hardly seemed worthy.
Edmonds had troubled him and had Bob Taylor been up to his
usual high standard behind the stumps, Richards may have been
dismissed.

At lunch England's hopes were high. In the hour after lunch
they evaporated. Richards was now at his magnificent best and
Collis King revealed himself in one of the greatest attacking
innings that can ever have been seen at international level. In
cold statistics they put on 139 for the fifth wicket in only
seventy-seven minutes, but these figures give little indication of
the glory of the hour.

King received sixty-seven balls and scored 86 runs. In an
innings of great excitement and tremendous power he hit three
mighty sixes and ten fours. There was not the slightest element
of luck nor of technical profanity in King's innings. He drove
with immense force. He pulled and hooked with disdainful

belligerence. His innings was breathtakingly beautiful in the
enormity of its strength and the manner of its execution.

To the eternal credit of the captain and the players, the
England fielding did not slip from its highest standard, but the
tactical error brought about by the original selection was
England's undoing. In the first twenty overs Brearley had used
five bowlers. After lunch he was forced to turn first to Boycott,
then to Gooch and Larkins. The twelve overs that these three
occasional bowlers sent down between them conceded 86
runs.

In the fifty-first over King swung Edmonds high to square-leg
and Randall took a fine catch on the boundary rope. In the
following over Richards reached his century. After those early
minutes of uncertainty it had become an inevitability. Since
lunch he had been in total command, dismissing the ball with
regal arrogance to all parts of the field. There is no-one who can
bowl to the man when the mood is upon him.

Murray, Roberts, Garner, Holding and Croft scored only five
runs between them in the final dash for runs. Irrelevant wickets
fell. The final gesture belonged to Richards. The last ball of the
innings was bowled by Hendrick. He aimed a yorker on off-
stump. Outguessing him, Richards stepped outside his off-
stump and lifted the ball over the leg-side boundary for his third
six. He also hit eleven fours and his innings had lasted just under
three and a half hours. It was majestic stuff.

Boycott and Brearley gave England a very solid start, essential
if England were to come anywhere near the target of 287. It is
worth reflecting that at lunch the West Indies had been 125 for
4 from thirty-four overs; the twenty-six overs of the afternoon
had produced 161 runs, more than six an over.

The England openers batted with great determination, but
they never got on top of the bowling. The overs ebbed away. It
took Boycott seventeen overs to reach double figures. They
were still together at tea and England had their platform for the
assault on the bowling that was necessary if victory was to be
achieved, but the assault never came. Even Richards, the fifth
bowler, escaped lightly.

In the thirty-fourth over, with the score at 107, Boycott
lofted a simple catch to Lloyd at mid-on. He contorted himself
into unnecessary difficulties and dropped it. There were those

among us who believed he was applying Machiavellian principles to keep Boycott at the wicket.

Whatever else Boycott and Brearley had done, they had silenced the West Indian supporters. The improvised steel bands had ceased to beat out their rhythms. But still the increase in the tempo of the batting did not come.

Brearley was out in the thirty-eighth over. The score was 128. Brearley swung Holder high to square-leg where Collis King took a catch similar to the one with which he himself had been dismissed. It had been a courageous opening stand, but the rest of the England batsmen had been left the task of scoring at well over seven runs an over against the bowling of Garner, Holding, Croft and Roberts — an impossible quest.

Two overs after Brearley's dismissal Boycott went and now there was a brief, glorious attack. Randall swiped until he swiped once too often and Gooch gave a glint of hope that the impossible could be achieved.

He hit Garner high to the mid-on boundary and pulled and drove with great power. In thirty-one minutes he received only twenty-eight balls and lashed 32 runs. If only the task had been smaller or he had come to the wicket earlier!

Gooch was bowled by Garner, the ball kept very low. Gower tried too much too soon, he had no alternative. Larkins went first ball, as did Taylor. It was a mercifully quick death for the rest. Garner took five wickets in eleven balls and finished with 5 for 38 — he was twice on a hat-trick.

The amateur tin bands were now at their noisiest as the West Indies rolled on to victory. The margin of 92 runs will for ever look a large one, but this was a wonderful game of fluctuating fortune in which, at three separate periods in the match, England had looked to be moving to success. There were self-inflicted wounds from the England side and selectors, but the same men also contributed much to the glories of the memorable day.

Richards took the Man-of-the-Match award although Garner and King had run him very close. Richards bowled tightly and took a marvellous running catch to dismiss Botham.

There was the opening stand of Boycott and Brearley which had temporarily silenced the West Indian supporters and there was a brilliant running catch by Brearley on the mid-on boundary. There was the fielding of Randall and Edmonds, and the power and the calm of Gooch. In short, there was cricket of the highest quality in every department of the game throughout a long and glorious day.

ENGLAND *v* WEST INDIES
Prudential World Cup Final
at Lord's
23 June 1979

West Indies

C.G. Greenidge	run out	9
D.L. Haynes	c Hendrick, b Old	20
I.V.A. Richards	not out	138
A.I. Kallicharran	b Hendrick	4
C.H. Lloyd (capt)	c and b Old	13
C.L. King	c Randall, b Edmonds	86
• D.L. Murray	c Gower, b Edmonds	5
A.M.E. Roberts	c Brearley, b Hendrick	0
J. Garner	c Taylor, b Botham	0
M.A. Holding	b Botham	0
C.E.H. Croft	not out	0
Extras	b 1, lb 10	11
	(for 9 wkts)	286

	O	M	R	W
Botham	12	2	44	2
Hendrick	12	2	50	2
Old	12	—	55	2
Boycott	6	—	38	—
Edmonds	12	2	40	2
Gooch	4	—	27	—
Larkins	2	—	21	—

fall of wickets
1—22, 2—36, 3—55, 4—99, 5—238, 6—252, 7—258, 8—260, 9—272

England

J.M. Brearley (capt)	c King, b Holding	64
G. Boycott	c Kallicharran, b Holding	57
D.W. Randall	b Croft	15
G.A. Gooch	b Garner	32
D.I. Gower	b Garner	0
I.T. Botham	c Richards, b Croft	4
W. Larkins	b Garner	0
P.H. Edmonds	not out	5
C.M. Old	b Garner	0
• R.W. Taylor	c Murray, b Garner	0
M. Hendrick	b Croft	0
Extras	lb 12, w 2, nb 3	17
		194

	O	M	R	W
Roberts	9	2	33	–
Holding	8	1	16	2
Croft	10	1	42	3
Garner	11	–	38	5
Richards	10	–	35	–
King	3	–	13	–

fall of wickets
1–129, 2–135, 3–183, 4–183, 5–186, 6–186, 7–188, 8–192, 9–192

West Indies won by 92 runs

ESSEX v SURREY

BENSON AND HEDGES CUP FINAL

At Lord's

21 July 1979

There can never again be any success quite as good as the first. It is surrounded by a romance, an innocent charm which can never be repeated. If success has been long in coming, then that moment of attainment is doubly sweet, for with it there comes a maturity like the end of innocence.

Essex waited one hundred and three years for success, and when it came at last, on a glorious day in July, at Lord's, there were few who begrudged them. This may seem hard on their opponents, Surrey, but that is the way of the world.

For some years, since Brian Taylor had first shaped an exuberant, exciting, talented, but temperamental side, Essex had threatened to win one of the four trophies. Twice they had been denied the John Player League by the narrowest of mathematical margins, and they had been deprived of a place in the Gillette Cup final by Somerset losing fewer wickets.

A collapse against Kent in the Gillette Cup at Leyton in 1972, and a collapse against the same county in the Benson and Hedges semi-final at Canterbury in 1973 had confirmed the suspicion that, in spite of the talent, there was a lack of conviction, of self-belief, in this side, that they were at their most excitable at the time when it was necessary to be most calm.

But a hardness developed. The young squires grew into tested warriors. Taylor had gone, but in his place was a captain of shrewdness and unsuspected sternness. Under Fletcher's leadership, they had chased Kent hard for the Schweppes County Championship in 1978, and they had been taught to believe that they could win. The arrival of Mike Denness was a most important contributory factor in that belief.

They began the 1979 season well, and they were to maintain their fine form to the end of the most memorable year in their history. In the qualifying competition of the Benson and Hedges Cup, they had narrowly beaten Northamptonshire, lost to Surrey, overwhelmed Combined Universities and comfortably accounted for Sussex.

In the quarter-final, a stunning century by Graham Gooch gave them victory over Warwickshire, and then they beat Yorkshire in an emotional semi-final with only one over and three wickets to spare.

Ironically, the side that they were to meet in the final was the one side that had beaten them in the competition.

Surrey had surprised most people by reaching the final. At the end of 1978, they had seemed to be in desolate disarray, but Mickey Stewart had become manager and taken them by the scruff of the neck and made them become a cricket team in keeping with the honourable traditions of the county, and he set them targets to strive for.

On the day of the final Lord's was a place of festivity, bubbling under a clear sky, baked in glorious sunshine. There was a general atmosphere of well-being, of friendly rivalry, as stranger greated stranger warmly, drawn together by the pervading good humour. A gentle breeze reduced the heat to comfort. The Essex supporters outnumbered their Surrey counterparts by five to one, sometimes it seemed more, and by ten-thirty in the morning, the stalls by the Grace Gates had sold every one of their Essex rosettes.

Roger Knight won the toss and put Essex in. Presumably he followed the contemporary belief that if the Lord's wicket 'did anything', it would 'do a bit' at the start of the day. He was influenced, too, by injuries which had deprived Surrey of Clarke and Thomas and left them handicapped by having Jackman far from fully fit.

Fletcher welcomed Knight's decision. Essex had made a tactical, but not unexpected, selection when Mike Denness was brought in for Alan Lilley. It had been Essex policy to play Lilley in the one-day matches and he had responded with marvellously aggressive knocks against Combined Universities and Sussex in which game he had won the gold award.

The jungle telegraph of first-class cricket had then begun to whisper words of vulnerability outside the off-stump and he had been out for nought in both the quarter-final and the semi-final.

It was hard on an exciting young player, but the experienced calm of Mike Denness was desperately needed.

Denness said afterwards that in all of his career he had never heard a roar so great as the one which greeted him and Graham Gooch as they came down the pavilion steps at Lord's to begin the Essex innings.

It was Denness who stroked the first four of the day through the off-side field and the roar of approval swept across the noble arena once again. Twenty-one runs came in the first three overs, gracious and powerful drives by the two openers. Roger Knight came on to halt the flow of runs, but after eleven overs the score was 48 and Essex were very much in charge. Then Denness, who had played quite beautifully, drove a little casually at Wilson and was caught at cover. Wilson was charging in almost from the pavilion gate, but most of the time Gooch was driving him back to his starting point with languid ease.

Ken McEwan now joined Graham Gooch. McEwan's beauty of style, the effortless grace with which he despatches the ball to the boundary line all round the field, hides a temperament which makes the beginning of an innings a nerve-racking experience for him. He strode on to the field at Lord's that day in seeming confidence, yet inwardly he was in agony. The indication came when he slashed wildly at a couple of balls outside the off-stump, but then he played an off-drive and quickly composure, class and elegance asserted themselves.

Gooch and McEwan were confronted by some of the best bowling of the day as Intikhab joined Roger Knight in the attack and drew from the experience of forty-seven Tests to contain and challenge the batsmen.

The threat of curtailment stimulated Gooch to even greater, solid, purposeful aggression. He moved down the wicket to the medium pace of Knight and hit him high over the sight screen at the Nursery End. The initiative now passed completely to Essex. McEwan was playing with that upright nonchalance which makes him one of the most exciting and elegant of batsmen. He cover-drove two fours, hooked a third and pulled a fourth. The erratic Pocock was punished severely and was conceding runs at more than one per ball.

Gooch reached his fifty, but McEwan soon overtook him, his fifty coming off only 68 deliveries.

At lunch thirty-seven overs had been bowled and Essex were 166 for 1. Whatever beverage was sipped at lunch, it could not compare with the champagne we had tasted in the two hours that led up to the interval. Neither batsman had played anything but an orthodox stroke. It was one of the finest partnerships ever seen in limited-over cricket, and one can think only of the Richards—King partnership of a month earlier that stands comparison with it.

Shortly after lunch, with only six more runs added, the partnership came to an end. McEwan sliced a ball from Wilson to Richards behind the stumps. His innings had lasted for ninety-six minutes and his 72 had been scored off ninety-nine balls. The stand had realised 124, a record for the competition and a lasting joy to all those who saw it. The runs had been scored in twenty-eight overs.

If Surrey had felt that their trials had ended with the dismissal of McEwan, they quickly realised that there was to be no respite.

When, after a long and distinguished career, a player finds himself in a cup final for the first time he draws to him a natural sympathy and good wishes for there is always the thought that this long-awaited chance of glory will never come again. Fletcher was received with great warmth. He had worked all his cricketing life for a day like this and he was determined to stamp his authority upon the game.

In years to come cricket lovers will read a simple statistic: Fletcher, bowled Knight, 34. Such brevity cannot convey the impact of an innings which lasted only thirty-seven minutes during which time the batsman received thirty balls. He hit three fours; one, a drive through mid-off off the back foot, was of such power and grace as to leave an image on the memory which will never fade. In the end he toppled over when he tried to cut Knight and was bowled. His innings had been a magnificent miniature.

The Surrey fielding had begun to wilt. One over from Robin Jackman, sadly unfit for such a contest as this, cost 17 runs. When Fletcher was out Essex were 239 for 3 and were on their way to their first ever honour in the grandest possible manner.

Throughout this time we had been savouring one of the very greatest innings ever played in a one-day match. On the eve of the match, Graham Saville, the Essex assistant secretary, had been asked what he thought Essex's chances of victory were. 'It all depends on Graham,' he said. 'If he can produce the goods, we're there.' What Gooch produced was not only the first century ever recorded in a Benson and Hedges final, but an innings of magnitude, personality and power. It had the strength of a century by Hammond and a range of shots that defies comparison.

As Wilson moved in off his marathon run Gooch sauntered down the wicket and flicked the ball off his toes into the crowd in the Mound Stand. Passively he repeated the shot, landing the ball on the roof of the stand. Viciously he pulled a four, the crowd scattering for safety as the ball parted them.

Hardie was out going for a big hit, but Pont helped to keep the momentum going. Then, with the score at 276 in the fifty-third over, Gooch swung with a grotesqueness totally out of context with the rest of his innings and was bowled by Wilson. He had scored 120, the highest score then reached in a Benson and Hedges final, and hit three sixes and eleven fours. His innings had lasted three hours, twenty minutes and as he left the field and disappeared up the pavilion steps the whole of the crowd rose to him with the consciousness that they had been in the presence of something mighty.

Phillip fell to the courageous Jackman and Essex closed on 290 for 6, a record for a Benson and Hedges final.

If Knight had considered his team's bowling to be a weakness, he certainly looked to their batting for strength. Alan Butcher had been in splendid form all summer and was to play in the final Test against India. Surrey looked to him to counterbalance Gooch's strength in the Essex side.

Opposed to Butcher and Lynch were Lever and Phillip. This was John Lever's golden year. In the month of June, stung by his non-inclusion in the England side for the Prudential World Cup, he had swept away all opposition. The duel between him and Butcher was seen as the crucial inner-contest of the match.

Butcher hit two fours and had scored 13 of the first 21 when Lever produced the ball of the match. It cut back sharply at the left-hander, took the inside edge of the bat and Smith gleefully accepted the catch.

Lynch had been preferred to the more sedate Clinton, but he

showed early signs of impatience. With East now operating from the Nursery End, Lynch drove fretfully at a good length ball and McEwan moved in from mid-off to take the catch.

Roger Knight now joined Geoff Howarth in a partnership which had to succeed if Surrey were to have any chance of victory. Without ever displaying the panache of the Essex batting, they nevertheless produced batting of quality which saw 91 runs added in eighteen overs. Incredibly, at the end of thirty overs they were ahead of Essex at the same stage.

Pont had come in for much punishment, but it was he who broke the third wicket stand. Knight, whose contribution to the Surrey side had been incalculable, drove hard at Pont, but the ball flew off the inside edge for Smith to take a wonderful catch, high and wide to his right.

David Smith immediately began to strike the ball, and when the usually so accurate Stuart Turner unwisely decided to attack Geoff Howarth's leg-stump, the New Zealander hit him for fourteen in the over.

The Essex fielding was still of a very high standard, but Fletcher was now needing to calm his excited troops.

At this point Howarth's tactics can be criticised although criticism comes easier if you are not in the heat of the middle. Over one hundred runs were still needed, but there was eighteen overs left and runs were coming without the need to resort to suicide.

Lever was brought back from the Nursery End with the sole purpose of trying to dismiss Howarth. He dropped one short and Howarth hooked high to Mike Denness at fine-leg, but the catch was missed. Disregarding the warning. Howarth pulled wildly at Pont and the ball bounced into the crowd, having escaped being caught by the narrowest of margins. He tried the shot again and the ball soared into the air with Fletcher, in closer at mid-on to save the single, poised under it for a seemingly interminable length of time. He clutched it safely to his chest.

Phillip produced a snorter for David Smith, but at 205 for 5 in the forty-second over, Surrey were still ahead of Essex at the same point.

Roope, surely batting too low at number six, produced some good shots and still Surrey lived. Much depended upon the aggressive Intikhab, but he fell to a fine catch by Pont, running round and in on the mid-on boundary. The limping Jackman was bowled by East.

Compensating for his earlier waywardness, Turner bowled a vital maiden to Roope and then, his calf muscles cramping with accumulated tension, he beat Richards' forward push and scattered his stumps.

Roope hit one majestic six into the Mound Stand and Surrey needed 44 from five overs with he and Pocock together. Pocock was bowled by Phillip.

Now Essex knew they had won. They waited only for the final confirmation. Lever at the Nursery End is bowling to Wilson. Wilson pushes forward and Lever punches the air as the stumps are knocked askew. Then the players race to the pavilion as the crowds pour over the boundary boards.

Trevor Bailey, with undisguised joy for his old county, pronounces Graham Gooch Man-of-the-Match and names this as the greatest of all Benson and Hedges finals. 544 runs in the day and some brilliant out-cricket would support his judgement.

ESSEX *v* SURREY
Benson and Hedges Cup Final
at Lord's
21 July 1979

Essex

M.H. Denness	c Smith, b Wilson	24
G.A. Gooch	b Wilson	120
K.S. McEwan	c Richards, b Wilson	72
K.W.R. Fletcher (capt)	b Knight	34
B.R. Hardie	c Intikhab, b Wilson	4
K.R. Pont	not out	19
N. Phillip	c Howarth, b Jackman	2
S. Turner	not out	1
*N. Smith		
R.E. East		
J.K. Lever		
Extras	b 3, lb 8, w 1, nb 2	14
	(for 6 wkts)	290

	O	M	R	W
Jackman	11	—	69	1
Wilson	11	1	56	4
Knight	11	1	40	1
Intikhab	11	—	38	—
Pocock	11	—	73	—

fall of wickets
1—48, 2—172, 3—239, 4—261, 5—273, 6—276

Surrey

A.R. Butcher	c Smith, b Lever	13
M.A. Lynch	c McEwan, b East	17
G.P. Howarth	c Fletcher, b Pont	74
R.D.V. Knight (capt)	c Smith, b Pont	52
D.M. Smith	b Phillip	24
G.R.J. Roope	not out	39
Intikhab Alam	c Pont, b Phillip	1
R.D. Jackman	b East	1
* C.J. Richards	b Turner	1
P.I. Pocock	b Phillip	7
P.H.L. Wilson	b Lever	0
Extras	b 4, lb 16, w 1, nb 5	26
		255

	O	M	R	W
Lever	9.4	2	33	2
Phillip	10	—	42	3
East	11	1	40	2
Turner	11	1	47	1
Pont	10	—	67	2

fall of wickets
1—21, 2—45, 3—134, 4—187, 5—205, 6—219, 7—220, 8—226, 9—250

Essex won by 35 runs

WARWICKSHIRE v HAMPSHIRE

JOHN PLAYER LEAGUE

At Edgbaston

29 July 1979

Sunday, 29 July 1979, was not a particularly good day for cricket. Seven John Player League games were scheduled for that day, but the matches at Folkestone and The Oval were abandoned without a ball being bowled, and the Worcestershire—Leicestershire game at Leicester was ended abruptly by rain when the visitors were in a good position.

The matches that were played were mostly restricted by the weather and had little relevance to the outcome of the league title. Middlesex, Essex and Glamorgan won their games without receiving much comment, but there were events at Edgbaston which did make people take notice.

A Sunday league fixture between Hampshire and Warwickshire at that time had little to commend it. Hampshire had won the league in 1978, but now they were in a process of restructuring their side. Barry Richards and Andy Roberts had gone, so too had Richard Gilliat, and the club was facing a period of readjustment under Bob Stephenson.

Warwickshire were in a terrible plight. They were struggling in the Schweppes County Championship; only Derbyshire and Glamorgan finished below them. And they went into this John Player League game with only two points to their name, obtained when the game against Derbyshire at Nuneaton was abandoned. They did not win a Sunday league match until the 5th August and they remained cemented at the bottom of the table to the end of the season.

In indifferent weather the fixture between these two sides was unlikely to have people clamouring for admission.

The match started on time and Gordon Greenidge and John Rice came out to open the Hampshire innings against the bowling of Hopkins and the ever reliable Steve Perryman. It was an uneventful beginning, suggesting nothing of the excitement and fury that was to come.

Greenidge was having a fine season. Rice was his regular
opening partner, but he still gave no indication that he had won
a permanent place in the side and there were some promising
young men waiting their turn and performing well in the second
eleven.

Greenidge got off the mark with a single from Hopkins'
second delivery. Rice played out the rest of the over. Greenidge
took a single off the fourth ball of Perryman's first over and
Rice opened his score with a four off the next ball.

Hopkins and Perryman bowled the first ten overs and conceded 44 runs. It was steady stuff for the Sunday league, par for
the course without hint of fireworks.

Phil Oliver with his medium pace and Chris Clifford, the
Yorkshire born off-break bowler, were the next pair into the
attack. There was still no indication of unrestrained aggression
until in the fifteenth over Greenidge hit Oliver for two huge
sixes. Whitehouse immediately replaced Oliver with Anton
Ferreira who began with a maiden to Rice. At the end of
twenty overs, the half-way stage, Hampshire were 82 for no
wicket. Greenidge was 40 not out.

Gradually the tempo increased. Ferreira's maiden opening
over proved to be the only maiden over of the match. Clifford
had bowled economically, concentrating on a flat trajectory on
or around leg-stump, but when he erred in direction he was
pulled for six and driven for four. Oliver returned to the attack
in place of Clifford.

In the twenty-sixth over, with the score on 122, Rice was
caught off Oliver. Greenidge was now in top gear. His last eleven
scoring shots had produced 44 runs, but now with Warwickshire's
emphasis entirely on defence, he was taking a single from nearly
every ball he received, occasionally piercing the far flung field
or driving over it for a violent four or six.

He and Turner added 38 in fourteen minutes. Turner hit two
fours in his 13. Jesty was in for eleven minutes while 13 runs
were scored of which he made one.

With Oliver having been severely punished, Whitehouse
brought Andy Lloyd on for an over. Greenidge hit him for 2, 6,
2, 6 and 1 off the first five balls, and Cowley took a single off
the last ball to make 18 from the over. It was, in fact, the only
over that Andy Lloyd bowled in limited-over cricket that summer.

Ferreira's last over, the thirty-seventh, produced 14 runs and a wide. The next over from Clifford saw only 3 runs scored, then, in the penultimate over of the innings, Oliver was hit for 14.

Cowley hit the first ball of the last over for six and was caught off the second ball when he tried to repeat the shot. He had batted for twenty-four minutes and scored 14, but his stand with Greenidge during that time had raised the score by 73 runs.

The batsmen had crossed when Cowley was caught so that Greenidge was able to take a single off the next ball. With only three balls of the innings left Terry went for a big hit and was caught. Again the batsmen had crossed so that Greenidge was able to take a two and a single off the last two balls.

The last four overs of the innings had produced 42 runs.

Gordon Greenidge had batted for two hours and eleven minutes and faced one hundred and twenty balls, exactly half the number bowled. His 163 not out was the highest innings ever played in the John Player League, beating by eight the record set up against Yorkshire by his team-mate Barry Richards. It meant that Greenidge held the record for the highest score in each of the three limited-over competitions. He had hit ten sixes and thirteen fours. It was the most sixes ever hit in the John Player League. Edgbaston is not a small ground.

As Warwickshire had not won a single game in the John Player League all season, they could have been forgiven for subsiding quietly after suffering Greenidge's onslaught and settling for an early night in preparation for the three-day championship game which was taking place against the same opponents at Nuneaton.

Amiss and Kallicharran had other ideas and against Marshall and Stevenson they began at a brisker rate than the Hampshire openers had done. The first wicket was worth 71 when Kallicharran was bowled by Taylor in the fourteenth over. It was a fine start, but it was nullified when Taylor dismissed Amiss upon whom much depended.

For victory it seemed that Warwickshire must have somebody to play a big innings. John Whitehouse promised with a flurry of aggression, but was caught behind off Rice. Oliver was instantly assured in his stroke-play and there was a useful stand with Lloyd.

It was Geoff Humpage, one of the hardest hitters in the game, who gave Warwickshire a positive chance of victory. First with the ebullient Oliver and then with Maynard, who was content to play a supporting role, he drove Warwickshire closer to their target.

With two overs remaining Warwickshire needed only 14 runs to win and they had four wickets in hand. Hampshire had nine fielders round the boundary in an effort to stop the runs.

Ferreira swung wildly and was lbw. Hopkins was caught behind in the last over and Humpage was left with the task of hitting four off the last ball to win the game for Warwickshire. He swung mightily and Turner, on the boundary, dived in an attempt to make a spectacular catch. He could not hold the ball, but he had stopped it crossing the boundary and Hampshire had won by one run.

WARWICKSHIRE *v* HAMPSHIRE
John Player League
at Edgbaston
29 July 1979

Hampshire

C.G. Greenidge	not out	163
J.M. Rice	c Humpage, b Oliver	43
D.R. Turner	b Perryman	13
T.E. Jesty	c Oliver, b Ferreira	1
N.G. Cowley	c Kallicharran, b Clifford	14
V.P. Terry	c Perryman, b Clifford	0
D.J. Rock	not out	0
M.N.S. Taylor		
* G.R. Stephenson (capt)		
M.D. Marshall		
K. Stevenson		
Extras	lb 11, w 3, nb 2	16
	(for 5 wkts)	250

	O	M	R	W
Hopkins	8	—	31	—
Perryman	8	—	32	1
Oliver	7	—	60	1
Clifford	8	—	44	2
Ferreira	8	1	49	1
Lloyd	1	—	18	—

fall of wickets
1–122, 2–160, 3–173, 4–246, 5–247

Warwickshire

D.L. Amiss	c Turner, b Taylor	41
A.I. Kallicharran	b Taylor	31
J. Whitehouse (capt)	st Stephenson, b Rice	22
P.R. Oliver	b Stevenson	54
T.A. Lloyd	c Terry, b Jesty	11
G.W. Humpage	not out	56
• C.W. Maynard	b Marshall	5
A.M. Ferreira	lbw, b Jesty	7
D.C. Hopkins	st Stephenson, b Rice	0
C.C. Clifford	not out	2
S.P. Perryman		
Extras	b 5, lb 8, w 6, nb 1	20
	(for 8 wkts)	249

	O	M	R	W
Marshall	8	—	31	1
Stevenson	8	—	46	1
Rice	8	—	56	2
Taylor	8	—	45	2
Cowley	2	—	14	—
Jesty	6	—	37	2

fall of wickets
1—71, 2—82, 3—117, 4—161, 5—197, 6—219, 7—244, 8—247

Hampshire won by 1 run

Above: 'The Old Brigade' takes the field for the one-day match at the Oval in May, 1946, to celebrate the centenary of the famous ground. From left to right: Andy Sandham, Patsy Hendren, Tich Freeman, M. Tate, M. J. C. Allom and Percy Fender. (*Photo*: Central Press)

Below: Ted Dexter holds the Gillette Cup as Sussex become the first winners. From left to right: Les Lenham, Jim Parks, Alan Oakman, Graham Cooper, Ted Dexter, Richard Langridge, Tony Buss (half hidden), Ken Suttle, Ian Thomson, Don Bates and John Snow. (*Photo*: Sport & General)

Geoffrey Boycott features in this book on several occasions but in a
distinguished career has rarely batted better than in the 1965 Gillette Cup
final against Surrey, when he scored 146. (*Photo*: Patrick Eagar)

Above left: West Indies captain, Clive Lloyd, hitting a huge six off Dennis Lillee during his 102 in the West Indies win over Australia in the Prudential World Cup final at Lord's in 1975. (*Photo*: Ken Kelly)
Above right: Basil D'Oliveira, the limping hero of a lost cause. Worcestershire v Kent, Benson and Hedges final, 1976.
(*Photo*: Patrick Eagar)

Below: Mike Procter bowling in the spell in which he took a hat-trick in the Benson and Hedges Hampshire v Gloucestershire match at Southampton, 1977. (*Photo*: Patrick Eagar)

Prudential World Cup final, 1979. Greenidge is run out by Randall. Brearley, Taylor and Old join in the celebrations. The moment when England dreamed of victory. (*Photo*: Patrick Eagar)

Prudential World Cup final, 1979. The three men who shattered England's dream: Collis King (*above left*), Viv Richards (*above right*) and Joel Garner (*right*). (*Photos*: Adrian Murrell)

Above: Benson and Hedges Cup final, 1979 — a golden day and batting of th very highest quality from Graham Gooch (*left*) and Ken McEwan (*right*). (*Photos*: Patrick Eagar)

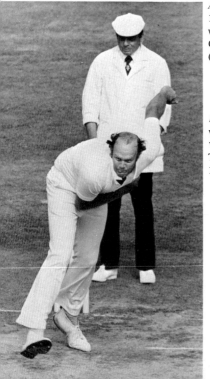

Left: Vincent van der Bijl. In his wonderful season with Middlesex he was involved in a statistical oddity at Taunton in the Benson and Hedges Cu 1980. (*Photo*: Patrick Eagar)

The aggressive batting of Mike Gatting came close to bringing
England victory in the Prudential Trophy match at Edgbaston, 1981, but
the final glory went to Geoff Lawson. (*Photo*: Patrick Eagar)

Above: Robin Jackman in characteristically buoyant mood after running out Trevor Chappell in a Prudential Trophy match. Jackman's all-round endeavour has been a dominant factor in Surrey's success in the one-day game in recent years. (*Photo*: Patrick Eagar)

Below: NatWest final, 1981. A Northamptonshire disaster: Allan Lamb is run out by Geoff Miller. Skipper Barry Wood looks on.
(*Photo*: Adrian Murrell)

SOMERSET v MIDDLESEX

BENSON AND HEDGES CUP

At Taunton

17 May 1980

When a game between two of the very best sides in the country produces 563 runs in a day and ends with victory off the last ball and only one run separating the two sides, there are few who would deny that it is entitled to be regarded as a great match.

Middlesex came to Taunton on 17 May 1980, knowing that whoever won their match against Somerset was virtually assured of a place in the quarter-finals of the Benson and Hedges Cup. It was sure to be a keen contest for here were two fine sides although it must be admitted that Somerset were a little below strength. Rose, the captain, was ill and unable to play and Botham, who led the side in Rose's absence, was not fit to bowl. They were, too, without Viv Richards and Joel Garner, the two West Indians who had done so much to lift Somerset to eminence in the cricket world.

As members of the West Indian side touring England they were unavailable for the county. Garner was sorely missed but to compensate for the absence of Richards, Somerset had signed Sunil Gavaskar, the great Indian batsman, on special registration for the year.

Middlesex had also taken advantage of the laws which allowed them to sign an overseas player on a year's contract and they had brought to England a player much less well known than Gavaskar. He was a friendly giant of a man from South Africa, a fast medium-pace bowler of relentless accuracy and subtle movement and a fierce hitter, Vincent van der Bijl. He was to play little part in shaping the outcome of this particular match although his year with Middlesex was to be a memorable one. His main contribution to this game was that he became involved in a statistical eccentricity.

Brearley and Mike Smith opened for Middlesex on a fast

pitch in fine weather, with an outfield encouraging the timed shot. An opening partner for Brearley was Middlesex's problem all season. Smith played less regularly. He was near the end of his fine career and was finding runs much harder to come by than in previous years. Middlesex were to solve their problems later in the season when Paul Downton was drafted into the side as an opener, but even then it proved to be only a temporary solution.

At Taunton, however, in May, it was Smith who was the more assured of the two openers. The score was 11 when Brearley touched Dredge to Denning. Radley, upon whom Middlesex were often so dependent, went immediately and when Smith fell to Jennings, Middlesex were struggling at 45 for 3.

This brought Barlow and Gatting together. Three days previously these two had come together in similar circumstances against Hampshire in the Benson and Hedges game at Southampton. They had added 166, a record fourth wicket stand for the competition, and won Middlesex the match by seven wickets. They now proceeded to save Middlesex again. With growing belligerence they added 163 before Barlow fell to Moseley, the most persistent of the Somerset bowlers.

Gould went quickly, but Phil Edmonds continued the attack on the Somerset bowling. In the last fifteen overs after lunch 126 runs were scored. The stand between Barlow and Gatting had been achieved in thirty overs and Barlow had hit fifteen fours and Gatting fourteen.

A target of 282 is a formidable one in any type of cricket; in fifty-five overs it looks very daunting. What was essential for Somerset was a good start and this is exactly what they had from Gavaskar and Denning.

Gavaskar was known to be a Test batsman of the very highest class, one whose name was mentioned in the same breath as Bradman, Richards, Compton, Hutton and others of that stature, but when Somerset signed him it was believed that, although he would be a great asset in the county championship matches, he was unlikely to prove very effective in limited-over cricket where the instant demands were out of character with his elegant, leisurely approach, bred in a country where time was not a vital factor.

He had quickly ended discussion as to his suitability for the one-day game when he and Rose had scored a record 241 for the first wicket against Kent in the Benson and Hedges match at Canterbury. Now, in his first 'home' Benson and Hedges game he gave a further indication of his powers. He hit three sixes and twelve fours in an innings of great majesty. He batted for 165 minutes. It was superb stuff and the opening stand of 120 with Peter Denning gave Somerset every chance of victory.

Denning was out when, in trying to force the pace, he lofted Edmonds to Daniel. Slocombe did not allow the tempo to slacken and was quickly giving Gavaskar the right support so that the score moved on briskly.

It was Phil Edmonds who bowled Middlesex back into the game. Never strictly adhering to the orthodox, ever ready for a challenge that quickens the intellect as well as the muscles, Edmonds is in most ways a cricketer out of his time. He is a reminder of the amateur who played hard, but for fun, and for whom boredom had no place in the game. There are those who would suggest that in these days when relentless professional efficiency is the dominating factor in the game Edmonds' approach borders on the dilettante. But this is to miss the point of the man. It confuses experiment with superficiality. Edmonds is rich in the first and will have none of the second. He is too committed to life.

At 217 he beat Gavaskar through the air and Gould stumped the Indian captain smartly. Then he had both Slocombe and Breakwell, a dangerous hitter, caught when they attempted more than the bowler. Edmonds also caught Botham off Selvey and Somerset were 229 for 5, and sinking.

The cricket now reached a feverish pitch. There was panic at the crease and more than a hint of panic in the field. The contestants were possessed by the game which was sweeping them along in a state of high excitement. Marks played a few power strokes and Taylor and Popplewell played the seamers with confidence as Somerset, always seeming to have a little too much to do, scurried towards their target.

The temperature of the game reached boiling point when Popplewell seemed to have been clearly run out, but as the fielders leapt in the air, umpire Peter Wight indicated that he had been unsighted and could not give the batsman out.

The excitement reached the scorers too. At the end of his unproductive spell Vincent van der Bijl retired to long leg and as he donned his sweater he turned to a boy in the crowd who had been scoring on the boundary line and asked, 'How many did I go for?'

The boy totted up van der Bijl's analysis and replied, 'Fifty-four.'

'Yes,' said van der Bijl, 'I thought I had taken some stick today.'

When the bowling analyses were published at the end of the game van der Bijl was shown as having been hit for 42 in his eleven overs. 'Blimey,' he remarked, 'that kid must have been a lousy scorer.'

Victor Isaacs, that relentless pursuer of statistical accuracy, heard this story and checked the score books with the two official scorers. They discovered that overs by Daniel and van der Bijl had been transposed and that the boy's analysis of 11−1−54−0 was indeed the right one. The score sheet printed here is, to my knowledge, the only correct one to have been published. The figures given in the form charts in *Pelham Cricket Year, 1980*, are right, but the bowling analyses given in *Wisden 1981* are incorrect. A bizarre interlude which reflects the pitch of excitement that the game had reached as it drew to its close.

With three overs to go Somerset needed 17 to win and had four wickets in hand. In the scamper for runs Taylor was run out after a valiant innings.

Jennings, too, was run out off the first ball of the final over so that Somerset needed ten runs to win off five balls. Popplewell and Dredge swung and sprinted, but four were needed off the last ball. Against a far flung field this was a difficult task and although the ball was hit hard into the outfield there were never more than two runs to be had.

Middlesex had won by one run and the Somerset supporters, even in their disappointment, joined in the acclaim.

In a match which had produced 563 runs in 110 overs the gold award went to a slow left-arm bowler. Edmonds had dismissed four front-line batsmen at a personal cost of 45 runs. He had also hit 32 quick and invaluable runs and caught the mighty Ian Botham. His gold award had been well earned against the claims of Gavaskar, Gatting, Barlow, Denning and Slocombe and the others who had contributed so much to this memorable match.

SOMERSET *v* MIDDLESEX
Benson and Hedges Cup
At Taunton
17 May 1980

Middlesex

J.M. Brearley (capt)	c Denning, b Dredge	6
M.J. Smith	c Botham, b Jennings	13
C.T. Radley	lbw, b Dredge	0
G.D. Barlow	c Slocombe, b Moseley	93
M.W. Gatting	not out	95
*I.J. Gould	c Denning, b Moseley	7
P.H. Edmonds	c Denning, b Moseley	32
J.E. Emburey	not out	5
V.A.P. van der Bijl		
M.W.W. Selvey		
W.W. Daniel		
Extras	b 4, lb 21, w 5, nb 1	31
	(for 6 wkts)	282

	O	M	R	W
Moseley	11	2	39	3
Dredge	11	—	59	2
Popplewell	8	1	42	—
Jennings	11	2	39	1
Breakwell	7	1	31	—
Marks	7	—	41	—

fall of wickets
1—11, 2—11, 3—45, 4—208, 5—218, 6—264

Somerset

S.M. Gavaskar	st Gould, b Edmonds	123
P.W. Denning	c Daniel, b Edmonds	42
P.A. Slocombe	c Emburey, b Edmonds	42
I.T. Botham (capt)	c Edmonds, b Selvey	3
D. Breakwell	c Daniel, b Edmonds	4
V.J. Marks	c Radley, b Daniel	10
D.J.S. Taylor	run out	21
N.F.M. Popplewell	not out	13
K.F. Jennings	run out	0
C.H. Dredge	not out	3
H.R. Moseley		
Extras	b 3, lb 6, w 3, nb 8	20
	(for 8 wkts)	281

	O	M	R	W
Daniel	11	3	32	1
van der Bijl	11	1	54	—
Selvey	8	—	64	1
Emburey	11	—	49	—
Edmonds	11	—	45	4
Gatting	3	—	17	—

fall of wickets
1–120, 2–217, 3–220, 4–227, 5–229, 6–254, 7–268, 8–273

Middlesex won by 1 run

ESSEX v SURREY

GILLETTE CUP QUARTER-FINAL

At Chelmsford

30 July 1980

Essex began the 1980 season as favourites in all four competitions. Their double success in 1979 had given them a confidence which added a dimension to their game. They now found themselves in the unfamiliar position of being expected to win when previously they had been consistent underdogs.

They had eased into the final of the Benson and Hedges Cup where they had looked to be beating Northamptonshire for three quarters of the game, only to end up losing by six runs in spite of some mighty hitting by Norbert Phillip at the close. Nine days after this disappointment they met Surrey in the quarter-finals of the Gillette Cup.

Surrey, it was considered, would be no problem to the men of Essex. Essex had beaten them in the Benson and Hedges final in 1979 and always appeared to have the better of the south Londoners in limited-over contests. With hopes of winning the John Player League and the Schweppes County Championship already fading, Essex saw the tie with Surrey as their last chance to win something during the season. They were confident, but not complacent.

Surrey were an efficient side who had been revitalised by the management of Mickey Stewart and the captaincy of Roger Knight. They had a large pool of players and there was healthy competition for first team places which were given on form. As a side they lacked panache, but they had been set targets to attain and they were working hard to achieve them.

It was, in fact, the fifth time that the sides had met during the season. Essex had won conclusively in both the John Player League and the Benson and Hedges Cup and had also had a convincing win in the Schweppes County Championship game at Chelmsford. Surrey's sole success had been on a dubious wicket in the return game at The Oval. The signs favoured Essex.

Surrey batted first in somewhat sultry conditions and they were soon in trouble. Phillip had not been able to settle and

Fletcher replaced him with Gooch. The atmosphere was right
for Gooch's swing and he had Butcher, the batsman Essex most
feared, caught by Denness. Eight runs later Roger Knight was
lbw to John Lever and Essex had scented victory with the game
barely half an hour old.

Howarth fretted impatiently, but he survived and stayed
while 39 were added. Clinton, whose range of strokes had
blossomed since he left Kent for Surrey, was batting with good
sense and a command of the difficult situation. He found a
good partner in the inelegant, but effective, Smith and they
added 73.

The all left-arm combination of East and Lever then brought
about a collapse and three wickets went down for 17 runs. It
was Robin Jackman who gave Surrey fresh hope with a vigorous
knock of 26. He received good support from Thomas and
Clarke, but Surrey's 195 for 7 was hardly a daunting score and
Essex bowlers felt, with complete justification, that they had
done their task well and that the batsmen should be able to
make the required runs without difficulty.

The belief that the bowlers would be able to spend the rest of
the afternoon sitting with their feet up on the balcony of the
Chelmsford pavilion was soon destroyed. The beginning of the
Essex innings was a nightmare.

This was Robin Jackman's year and the wholehearted all-
rounder was determined that it would be his day too. He is an
eager cricketer who breathes his love of the game with constant
endeavour. The cruelty of his entry into Test cricket was still a
few months away, but even when that troublesome time came
he accepted it with dignity and humour and it quickened his
appetite for the game even more.

He tore into the Essex batting and moved the ball about
disconcertingly. Knight gave admirable support and in fifteen
overs Essex lost Gooch, Denness, McEwan and Fletcher, the
strongest first four in the country, for 35 runs. The Chelmsford
crowd was stunned to an embarrassed silence and the ground
took on the air of mourning for defeat. Brian Hardie had other
ideas. Here was a situation his granite personality relished and in
Keith Pont, a young man of immense talent that has not always
been well used by team selectors, he found a solid partner.

Hardie is one of cricket's great characters, a man for all

seasons, one able to adjust to any emergency. He is a fighter and
one of good sense and good humour. He analyses his own game
and knows what he can and cannot do and he structures his
game accordingly. He is a rock in the middle of the Essex order,
but a rock which can generate sparks when the weather is
favourable.

He and Pont took the score to 100. There was a splendid
spell of bowling from Pat Pocock who had had some uneasy
moments in the limited-over game, but chose this day for one of
his finest performances though one that went unrewarded with
a wicket. Knight was forced to bring himself and Jackman back
into the attack to break the Pont—Hardie stand. It was the
captain himself who took the vital wicket when he had Pont
caught behind and then Jackman quickly removed Stuart
Turner, a most valuable wicket for here is one of the great one-
day players.

'Nobby' Phillip joined Hardie and the ball began to fly
around the ground as the West Indian continued in the same
vein as that which he had shown at Lord's in the Benson and
Hedges final less than a fortnight earlier.

The fifty-fourth over of the innings was bowled by Sylvester
Clarke and Hardie and Phillip took 17 runs from it. This meant
that Essex needed only 11 runs to win and that they had six
overs in which to get them with four wickets still standing. The
crowd was now roaring happily for the scent of victory was
very strong.

When Hardie lofted Jackman rather lazily to Butcher at mid-
on in the next over it seemed only a temporary upset. It was a
pity Hardie had not stayed until the end for he had batted quite
magnificently and it was on him that the Essex victory surely
had been founded.

Ray East was at the wicket now with Phillip and six runs
were scored with little need for haste or heroics. There were now
three overs left and only five runs were needed with three
wickets standing. It was a time for calm and consideration, but it
was now that fever could be sensed in the air. It gripped East.
He called Phillip for an impossible run and the West Indian was
run out by yards — a sad, sad waste. There was unease in the
Essex camp for temperament was failing and ghosts from the
past were abroad on the ground.

Smith swung lustily for one and then he hit airily and nervously at Clarke and was bowled. 193 for 9. Three runs still needed.

John Lever took a single and then Robin Jackman in a supreme effort of accuracy bowled a maiden to him so that Essex started the last over needing two runs to win.

The odds were still in their favour. In an effort to snatch victory when Hardie, Pont and Phillip were moving the balance towards Essex, Roger Knight had brought back his front-line bowlers earlier than he would have wanted to do in normal circumstances. This meant that of his five bowlers only David Thomas was able to bowl the last over.

A left-arm medium pace bowler, Thomas was the youngest and least experienced member of the Surrey side. He had received a terrible mauling earlier in the afternoon when his first eleven overs had conceded 55 runs. If Essex could have chosen, they would have selected Thomas to bowl the last over to them. The young man himself could have hardly relished the situation.

Ray East turned away his first ball and the batsmen crossed for an easy single. The scores were level. To their credit Surrey still believed that they could win and played and fielded in that belief. Thomas to Lever. Three balls are straight and John Lever pushes forward in his rather hunched defensive stroke. There are now two balls of the match remaining and victory is still a possibility for either side.

On the penultimate ball of the over Lever played the ball out to mid-off and suddenly, as if programmed to self-destruct, East is seen charging down the wicket. Roger Knight's under-arm throw beats him to the wicket and the Surrey players leap in the air in joy of a victory so unexpected. For Essex there is shock and a sense of bewilderment. There is also an awareness that they have lived through this before. Little did they realise then that they were to live through it again in twelve months' time. Only the venue would be changed, and the opposition.

ESSEX *v* SURREY
Gillette Cup Quarter-Final
at Chelmsford
30 July 1980

Surrey

A.R. Butcher	c Denness, b Gooch	8
G.S. Clinton	c McEwan, b East	58
R.D.V. Knight (capt)	lbw, b Lever	2
G.P. Howarth	c Fletcher, b Gooch	19
D.M. Smith	c Phillip, b East	37
G.R.J. Roope	c Hardie, b Lever	4
D.J. Thomas	b Lever	17
R.D. Jackman	not out	26
S.T. Clarke	not out	11
*C.J. Richards		
P.I. Pocock		
Extras	b 3, lb 10	13
	(for 7 wkts)	195

	O	M	R	W
Lever	12	4	26	3
Phillip	12	—	48	—
Gooch	12	1	44	2
Turner	12	1	36	—
East	12	1	28	2

fall of wickets
1—14, 2—19, 3—58, 4—131, 5—136, 6—148, 7—176

Essex

G.A. Gooch	b Jackman	11
M.H. Denness	c Thomas, b Jackman	1
K.S. McEwan	lbw, b Jackman	2
K.W.R. Fletcher (capt)	b Knight	9
B.R. Hardie	c Butcher, b Jackman	70
K.R. Pont	c Richards, b Knight	29
S. Turner	c and b Jackman	4
N. Phillip	run out	45
R.E. East	run out	4
*N. Smith	b Clarke	1
J.K. Lever	not out	1
Extras	b 6, lb 6, w 2, nb 4	18
		195

	O	M	R	W
Jackman	12	4	22	5
Clarke	12	1	47	1
Knight	12	3	35	2
Thomas	11.5	—	56	—
Pocock	12	5	17	—

fall of wickets
1—7, 2—18, 3—19, 4—35, 5—100, 6—108, 7—185, 8—191, 9—193

Surrey won on losing fewer wickets with scores level

DERBYSHIRE v YORKSHIRE

BENSON AND HEDGES CUP

At Derby

9 and 11 May 1981

The summer of 1981 began wet and cold. So cold was it at Fenner's, where Essex were playing Cambridge University in the opening match of the season, that the umpires suspended play for a while. The weather ravaged the early stages of the Benson and Hedges Cup. Northamptonshire, the holders, were eliminated more by not finding their way onto the field, than by being defeated, and Middlesex, the favourites, suffered a similar fate. Matches dragged on into the second day and a miserable time was had by all.

One of the matches that spilled over from the Saturday to the Monday was that between Derbyshire and Yorkshire at Derby. Both sides had struggled somewhat uneasily over the past few years. Yorkshire had replaced Boycott as captain by Hampshire who had now relinquished the post in favour of Old, but although there appeared to be talent in the side, there was an uneasy calm below the surface and, on occasions, their out-cricket was quite dreadful.

Derbyshire had prospered under the inspiring leadership of Eddie Barlow, but since his return to South Africa they, like Yorkshire, had flirted with captains. Bob Taylor had asked to be relieved of the position, and David Steele had come from Northants to lead the side. His tactics had been severely criticised in the press for their lack of aggression, and he had resigned to be succeeded by Geoff Miller. The effect of captaincy on Miller's form was to be catastrophic and before 1981 was through, he, too, was to give up the post. He had returned from the West Indies in April 1981, as vice-captain of England, but by the end of the English season he was to fade into obscurity, an obscurity redeemed by one memorable moment.

None of these thoughts preoccupied the players when they gathered at Derby on Saturday 9 May. Their immediate concern was to play some cricket in conditions which were damp and dull, and altogether uninviting. It was a murky day. Showers punctuated the play and the pitch was sullen and sluggish, and in the end only 59 of the allotted 110 overs were to be bowled before bad light put everyone out of his misery.

Chris Old won the toss and, probably in hope of better conditions to come, he asked Derbyshire to bat. Certainly he had no immediate reward. Miller himself opened with the New Zealander John Wright, Alan Hill being omitted in favour of Brooks.

Miller remains the great enigma of English batting. There are times when in poise, elegance and ease of stroke he looks to be a player of the very highest class, a two-thousand-runs-a-year man, with sixty centuries behind him. He has yet to hit a hundred in first-class cricket and as the years pass, it looks as if he never will attain the batsman's pinnacle of achievement. But here, with the ball coming laboriously onto the bat and the chance of strokes in anger eradicated, Miller dabbed and pushed to elegant effect. He was caught behind off Old when he had nudged 20 out of 27. Peter Kirsten then defied the conditions to score in a brisk manner. It was not easy to drive, but he was ever looking for runs, and he, like Miller, nudged to effect. He is so quick on his feet that even if his batting lacks the ultimate mark of exciting personality, he still accumulates runs at a good rate and gives pleasure.

At the other end, Wright was not entirely himself. Here surely is one of the world's very great players off the back foot, but when frustrated he charges down the wicket, out of character, and violating his strength. He survived with perseverance, and the hundred came up. He hooked Sidebottom for six and then was caught, slogging at Stevenson. 126 for 2.

Kirsten had been dropped at the wicket off Johnson, who was playing his first match, but generally the Yorkshire medium pacers were neither as economic, nor as effective as they should have been on this wicket. There was success for Yorkshire, however, when Kirsten played on to Johnson to give him a notable first wicket in senior cricket. And then Derbyshire drooped. Two were run out in the scramble for quick runs. Old's unrelenting accuracy had its reward, and five wickets fell for 41 runs. 202 for 8 was not as much as had looked possible, but, in the conditions, it was a most commendable score.

Yorkshire scored 12 in four overs before bad light meant that all had to return on Monday.

Derbyshire went to Old Trafford on the Sunday and beat Lancashire, and Yorkshire made a fruitless visit to Edgbaston where they sat and watched the rain. The general impression was that their visit to Derby on the Monday would also prove fruitless, Deryshire's total, it was felt, being substantial in the conditions.

Yorkshire gave credibility to this view with their early batting which was circumspect in the extreme. Athey went immediately to Wood. Chris Old appeared to attempt to break the control that the bowlers had gained. He struck a couple of lusty blows and then was concerned in an unprecedented incident.

Spotting that Derbyshire had only three, and not the requisite four, men fielding inside the inner fielding ring, thirty yards from the wicket, he swung wildly at Wood and had his stumps knocked back. To his surprise there was no call of 'no-ball' and he trudged complainingly back to the pavilion. He reiterated his claim that he was not out and a telephone call to Lord's and the TCCB proved that he was right and, after a ten-minute delay, he was reinstated. Evidently, only umpire Harold Bird had seen the infringement and he asked for the ruling that, in such circumstances, either umpire could call 'no-ball'.

Ironically, four overs later, for the addition of only three runs, Old was legitimately bowled by Wood. This was the least of Yorkshire's troubles. Against the left-arm of Tunnicliffe they crumbled. Play had not begun until 2.30 and the conditions were no more propitious than they had been on the Saturday. Before an understandably meagre crowd, on a ground that is not amongst the loveliest even when the sun shines, they were 123 for 9, and the game, seemingly was over.

Mark Johnson, the twenty-three-year-old captain of Holmfirth, came to the wicket to join David Bairstow who had come in with the score at 64 for 5.

Admittedly, the surface was now drier, the ball older and the movement less eccentric, but Johnson batted with a composure and good sense which had not been evident in the earlier batsmen. He concentrated on survival while Bairstow, with that unquenchable spirit that believes all is possible, went for victory.

David Bairstow is a cricketer of optimism and enthusiasm. He is not among the top rank of wicket-keepers, but he exudes energy in all that he does. He had returned from the West Indies, where his wicket-keeping had been severely criticised, with his Test career stifled at birth. Some would have wilted, but Bairstow is of stern stuff and he loves the game, and for him cricket is Yorkshire.

His attack was vehement. The fifth Derbyshire bowler was to be a combination of Steele and Miller. Steele had begun well enough, dismissing both Carrick and Sidebottom, but Bairstow was vicious. Steele, and Miller, who bowled one over, were hit for five sixes and Bairstow's fifty came in twenty-one overs.

There had been brought about a remarkable transformation in atmosphere. Six overs remained and Yorkshire needed 49 for victory, and the impossible seemed feasible.

Steele was still operating from the end which meant that he was bowling to a short leg-side boundary. Bairstow facing — 6, 4, 2, 2, 6, 6. Twenty-six runs in the over and Steele retired from the attack after conceding 70 runs in nine overs.

Sidebottom had little effect in halting the flow of runs and when Geoff Miller accepted the captain's responsibility of bowling the fifty-fourth over, only seven runs were needed for a Yorkshire victory.

Bairstow hit him over mid-wicket for six, the ninth of his innings, to reach a memorable hundred and Yorkshire had won with eight balls to spare.

Bairstow's second fifty had come in six overs (seventeen minutes). In all he batted for one hundred and eight minutes and hit three fours as well as his nine sixes. His previous highest score in the competition had been 35.

The last wicket stand of 80 was a record for the Benson and Hedges Cup, and Bairstow had scored all but four of them. These four had been scored by Mark Johnson, a seam bowler making his debut. A handful of spectators had watched one of the very great innings of limited-over cricket and, arguably, the most dramatic.

Yorkshire's victory gave them qualification to the quarter-finals of the competition. They lost to Somerset at that stage.

Mark Johnson took seven first-class wickets during the season. He took four wickets against Scotland in a Benson and Hedges match, but in other one-day games never more than one.

At the end of the season he was not retained, but he had shared his moment of glory, and his own contribution had been by no means insignificant.

DERBYSHIRE *v* YORKSHIRE
Benson and Hedges Cup
at Derby
9 and 11 May 1981

Derbyshire		
J.G. Wright	c Hartley, b Stevenson	47
G. Miller (capt)	c Bairstow, b Old	20
P.N. Kirsten	b Johnson	65
D.S. Steele	c Carrick, b Old	12
K.J. Barnett	run out	7
K.G. Brooks	run out	3
B. Wood	c Bairstow, b Old	10
C.J. Tunnicliffe	b Sidebottom	10
* R.W. Taylor	not out	14
M. Hendrick	not out	0
S. Oldham		
Extras	lb 8, nb 6	14
	(for 8 wkts)	202

	O	M	R	W
Old	11	—	33	3
Stevenson	11	—	43	1
Johnson	11	—	33	1
Sidebottom	10	—	33	1
Hartley	5	—	14	—
Boycott	3	—	16	—
Carrick	4	—	16	—

fall of wickets
1—27, 2—126, 3—155, 4—161, 5—165, 6—172, 7—178, 8—192

Yorkshire		
G. Boycott	b Tunnicliffe	31
C.W.J. Athey	c Kirsten, b Wood	4
C.M. Old (capt)	b Wood	15
J.D. Love	lbw, b Tunnicliffe	6
J.H. Hampshire	c and b Tunnicliffe	14
S.N. Hartley	c Steele, b Tunnicliffe	1
* D.L. Bairstow	not out	103
G.B. Stevenson	c Brooks, b Tunnicliffe	13
P. Carrick	st Taylor, b Steele	3
A. Sidebottom	c and b Steele	0
M. Johnson	not out	4
Extras	lb 6, w 1, nb 2	9
	(for 9 wkts)	203

	O	M	R	W
Hendrick	10	1	22	—
Tunnicliffe	11	3	24	5
Oldham	11	1	36	—
Wood	11	2	24	2
Steele	9	—	70	2
Miller	1.4	—	18	—

fall of wickets
1—19, 2—42, 3—61, 4—62, 5—64, 6—102, 7—115, 8—123, 9—123

Yorkshire won by 1 wicket

ENGLAND v AUSTRALIA

PRUDENTIAL TROPHY

At Edgbaston

6 June 1981

The limited-over game had been treated with scepticism by spectators and with indifference by players when it was first introduced to Australia. It was Mr Packer's organisation which first exploited its potential to the full, their enthusiasm for the commercial rewards of this type of cricket leading to an indigestible array of fixtures. It was still felt, however, that when it came to the one-day game England had the edge. In experience and tactics they were superior to the Australians who tended to treat the Prudential Trophy matches as a warm-up for the sterner encounters of the Tests to come.

There seemed nothing unusual in the approach to the Prudential Trophy games of 1981. The Australians had had a miserable start to the tour, being confined to the pavilion day after day as the rain lashed down. When they were beaten at Lord's in the first of the three Prudential Trophy games it surprised no one. The match produced few fireworks and England won with six wickets and more than three overs to spare. It was predictable stuff.

For the second encounter, at Edgbaston, the weather too was predictable, cold and grey with the suggestion that rain could stop proceedings at any moment.

Botham won the toss and asked Australia to bat. Wood began assertively, but Trevor Chappell was out to the first ball he received. He essayed a hook at a Botham long hop and was caught behind off his glove. Yallop, who had not played at Lord's in the first match, now joined Wood and, like Wood, was quickly into his stride. Willis and Hendrick bowled tightly, but runs still came at three an over.

With the score at 80 for 1 the rain came and but for the effective covering of the Edgbaston ground, could have ended play for the day. The system had been installed at Edgbaston in the previous winter and there had been some teething troubles, but as the engines from Finland rolled the covers off the three and a half acres of turf one could only hope that Warwickshire's brave innovation would be a success that would be adopted by grounds everywhere.

The lunch break was extended but as soon as the rain stopped, play was possible and the pitch perfectly dry. The break had done little good for Australia for, in the thirtieth over, with the score at 96, Wood's splendid innings came to an end. He was well caught by the sprawling Willis when he swung at Jackman.

Kim Hughes was majestic and authoritative from the start of his innings. He drove Willey high into the pavilion and dissected the cover field with the precision and sweetness that he had achieved in the Centenary Test at Lord's the previous summer, an occasion which, but for him, would have been very bleak indeed. At one time Hughes and Yallop were scoring at six runs an over. The end came when Hendrick, by far the best and most naggingly accurate of the England bowlers, knocked back Yallop's leg-stump in the last of his eleven overs. What followed was a mad scramble for runs.

Hughes was run out by a diving throw from Gower. Border hit Gooch for a mighty six over long-off and then was run out by Willey who hit the stumps from eighty yards. Marsh played some typically lusty shots before being caught on the boundary and then Australia gained an unexpected and vital bonus.

Botham had erred in his allotment of overs to his bowlers. England's fifth bowler was a combination of Gooch and Willey, and this combination conceded 74 runs in eleven overs. Unaccountably, Gooch found himself bowling the penultimate over and Geoff Lawson took full advantage of the fact with 14 runs in the over including a six lofted over extra cover and a six swung massively over mid-wicket.

England faced a total which was larger than they could have expected. It grew to stupendous proportions when, in the ninth over and only 20 runs scored, Hogg beat and bowled Gooch. Then Lawson bowled Boycott and Alderman bowled Gower, and England were 36 for 3.

Their position was bad, but it should have been worse. Before he scored, Gatting was dropped by Marsh, a straightforward catch to his right. Shortly after Gower was out, Gatting was dropped again. He edged the ball at waist height to Marsh off Alderman and the simplest of chances was put on the floor.

Gatting responded to this luck with some pugnacious shots. He had useful support from Love who, playing in only his second representative game, drove and cut well.

The interruption through rain had meant that tea was not taken until ten past six, and after tea Gatting and Love moved firmly into the attack. They were particularly severe on Trevor Chappell whose round arm medium pace held no problems. It seemed that they had wrested control from the Australians, but when their stand was worth 75 Love edged Lawson into his stumps.

Gatting was now in violent form, but Willey matched him run for run, pillaging 37 runs off forty balls. They added 66 before Willey fell to a fine diving catch in the covers by Wood.

Chappell was still suffering. Gatting hit him high into the pavilion and with ten overs left England were 188 for 5. Botham was hitting with great power and England appeared to be heading for victory.

They reduced the number of runs needed per over with some fine shots, but when he had scored 24 off thirty balls Botham skied Lawson and Hughes held another of the day's great catches as he fell backwards at mid-on. 224 for 6. 26 runs needed in five overs.

Geoff Humpage joined Gatting and the home crowd bubbled in expectant excitement that he could produce his Warwickshire form of virile batting and steer England to success. It was not to be. He fretted painfully. The fifty-second over was bowled by Hogg and Humpage, embarrassingly unable to make contact, conceded a maiden. In the next over he was bowled by Lillee when he moved away to slash the ball through the off-side. It was a sadly ugly finish.

With two overs remaining England needed sixteen to win. Mike Gatting's innings had grown in stature as it had lengthened in duration. Now it was in full splendour. He drove Hogg past mid-wicket for four and then hit a glorious cover-drive for another four, and England needed only six from the last over, which was to be bowled by Lillee.

The time was 8.30 as Dennis Lillee ran in to bowl the last

over amid great excitement. The excitement was not confined
to the spectators for, in the field, the Australians were in a state
of great agitation with gesticulations and resetting of the field
showing the tension and anxiety. Jackman pushed forward at
Lillee's first ball and Gatting called for the run. Lillee picked
up and hit the wicket with his throw and Jackman was run
out, but Gatting had the strike. 244 for 8. Six needed from five
balls.

Lillee moved in to bowl again. Gatting drove him, high and
mighty to mid-off. The crowd roared for what they believed
was another boundary, the four that would give Gatting his
hundred and put England within a grasp of taking the match.

Geoff Lawson was fielding on the boundary some twenty
yards from where Gatting had placed the ball. Sprinting round
the boundary, he dived and held the ball one-handed, inches
from the ground for a brilliant and historic catch. The distance
that Lawson had covered in reaching the ball made the brilliance
of the catch all the more commendable. There were those who
believed that in the history of international cricket it stood on a
par with Clem Hill's diving outfield catch at Old Trafford in
1902.

The crowd was stunned by the unexpected, but then roared
its approval of both batsman and fielder. There can have been
few great innings which have been brought to so glorious an end.

So six runs were needed off four balls and only Willis and
Hendrick to get them. At the moment of high drama we had
light comedy.

The local crowd gave their captain a tumultuous reception
when he drove Lillee to mid-off for a single off the third ball.
Five needed from three balls. Hendrick swung at the fourth ball
and it went off his pads. The stop and start running provided
the comedy. The Australians were not laughing. They were
too excited and an uncertain leg-bye was turned into two leg-
byes by an overthrow which had a touch of hysteria about it.

Three runs needed for an England victory, two balls to go,
the last pair at the wicket, and the demon bowler bowling.

Hendrick drove powerfully at the fifth delivery, but he
failed to get in line. The ball clipped the edge of the bat and
there was Marsh clasping the ball in his gloves, thankful that
after his early lapses he had held on to the one that mattered.

It was twenty minutes to nine and Australia had won by two runs. Gatting was named Man-of-the-Match although there were many heroes, not the least of whom was Geoff Lawson who took the wickets of Boycott, Love and Botham, scored 29 vital runs and held the finest catch that most people at Edgbaston that day had ever seen.

ENGLAND v AUSTRALIA
Prudential Trophy
at Edgbaston
6 June 1981

Australia

G.M. Wood	c Willis, b Jackman	55
T.M. Chappell	c Humpage, b Botham	0
G.N. Yallop	b Hendrick	63
K.J. Hughes (capt)	run out	34
A.R. Border	run out	17
* R.W. Marsh	c Love, b Botham	20
M.F. Kent	lbw, b Willis	1
G.F. Lawson	not out	29
D.K. Lillee	run out	8
R.M. Hogg	not out	0
T.M. Alderman		
Extras	b 1, lb 18, w 1, nb 2	22
	(for 8 wkts)	249

	O	M	R	W
Willis	11	3	41	1
Botham	11	1	44	2
Hendrick	11	2	21	1
Jackman	11	—	47	1
Willey	6	—	36	—
Gooch	5	—	38	—

fall of wickets
1—10, 2—96, 3—160, 4—171, 5—183, 6—193, 7—213, 8—248

England

G.A. Gooch	b Hogg	11
G. Boycott	b Lawson	14
M.W. Gatting	c Lawson, b Lillee	96
D.I. Gower	b Alderman	2
J.D. Love	b Lawson	43
P. Willey	c Wood, b Chappell	37
I.T. Botham (capt)	c Hughes, b Lawson	24
• G.W. Humpage	c Lillee	5
R.D. Jackman	run out	2
R.G.D. Willis	not out	1
M. Hendrick	c Marsh, b Lillee	0
Extras	lb 12	12
		247

	O	M	R	W
Hogg	11	2	42	1
Lillee	10.5	2	36	3
Alderman	11	1	46	1
Lawson	11	2	42	3
Chappell	11	–	69	1

fall of wickets
1–20, 2–27, 3–36, 4–111, 5–177, 6–224, 7–232, 8–244, 9–244

Australia won by 2 runs

NATIONAL WESTMINSTER BANK TROPHY — 1981

SEMI-FINALS AND FINAL

There was great regret at Gillette's decision to end their sponsor-ship of the sixty-over competition. It had been the first and arguably the best of the one-day tournaments, and cricket owed much to Gillette. That the competition would continue in the same form, but under the new name of the NatWest Trophy, could not disguise the fact that it needed to re-establish itself in the public interest. The cricketing world is a conservative one and a change, albeit only a name, is viewed with suspicion.

The NatWest Trophy lost no time in capturing the headlines. In the week before the Benson and Hedges final, Somerset, Surrey and Middlesex were all knocked out of the Nat West competition. There were signs of a Lancashire resurgence and hopes that the 'red rose' county could stamp their authority on the new trophy as they had done on the old in its early days.

Lancashire continued their success with victory over Hamp-shire in a poor quality game at Southampton. Along the coast at Hove, Essex beat Sussex, the favourites, in a wonderful game and became the side fancied to win the trophy. In the semi-final they were drawn to meet Derbyshire, suprising conquerors of the leading county, Nottinghamshire. The other semi-final brought together Lancashire and Northants.

In spite of the efforts at improvement, which have included the building of a new pavilion, the Northampton ground has yet to achieve that atmosphere of homeliness which accompanies success. Yet success there had been for Northamptonshire. They had reached the Gillette Cup final in 1979, won the Benson and Hedges Cup in 1980 and stood one game away from the first NatWest Trophy final. Their first five batsmen presented a formidable array of talent and the arrival of Neil Mallender had given their bowling a dimension which it had formerly lacked.

Lancashire were an experienced side and at times in the field looked positively ancient, but the development of Allott and the addition to the side of Michael Holding had made the bowling a powerful force with which to contend.

Geoff Cook won the toss and invited Lancashire to bat although the logic of this decision was hard to follow. There was immediate reward, however. Kennedy, having scored all of the first six runs, edged Sarfraz to slip where Yardley took a fine catch low down. Fowler and David Lloyd then made nonsense of any hint of crisis with an untroubled stand which took them to 110 at lunch off thirty-seven overs.

Fowler, in particular, played some fine shots and underlined his promise as a young batsman of genuine quality who might very soon represent his country. David Lloyd was rich in determination and good sense, and here seemed the ideal blend.

There appeared to be no reason why these two batsmen should not carry their success into the afternoon for both reached accomplished fifties, but in the fifth over of the afternoon David Lloyd drove a Williams off-break hard and straight to extra cover where Carter, who had come into the side for the injured Willey, took the catch. Two overs later Williams had Fowler caught behind and in the next over came the vital wicket for Northants when Sharp took a fine leg-side catch to dismiss Clive Lloyd off Tim Lamb, the West Indian captain trying to glance. Reidy was immediately leg-before to Tim Lamb and three wickets had fallen with the score at 123.

Abrahams became another Sharp/Tim Lamb victim and the slide continued. David Hughes, in his benefit year, had had a good season with the bat and for a while it looked as if he and Jack Simmons might restore sanity to the Lancashire batting. The big score which had seemed inevitable had gone with the dismissal of Clive Lloyd and the hopes of recovery went when Hughes, aiming to drive to long-off, was caught on the third man boundary by Tim Lamb. 110 for 1 after thirty-seven overs had turned to 144 for 7 from fifty-two.

Neither O'Shaughnessy nor Allott stayed long, but Holding helped Simmons with some mighty swings and the last wicket added 25 runs, runs which in the light of what happened later played a significant part in the shape of the match.

Northamptonshire had to make 187 to win, a score well within their capabilities on a wicket which had remained easy paced.

They began with assurance. Holding and Allott appeared to have been weathered and runs were accumulating, but just as the Northants supporters began to relax, Wayne Larkins, that elegantly aggressive batsman upon whom the gods have not smiled favourably at the top level, was lbw to Allott.

Williams made a very uncertain start, but he survived. He is a young cricketer of the very richest promise, but 1981 was not a vintage year for him. He and Cook took the score past fifty and then, incomprehensibly, Cook was bowled by the erratic O'Shaughnessy. If Lancashire could point to a failure in selection after the match, it must be in the decision to play O'Shaughnessy in preference to the seasoned Peter Lee.

Cook's dismissal brought Allan Lamb to the wicket and upon this man, above all others, rested the hopes of Northamptonshire. Williams was now batting with confidence and Lamb settled in quietly and efficiently. At tea, all was well.

In the second over after tea Allan Lamb was caught at backward short-leg off Jack Simmons and, one run later, in Simmons' next over, Williams was taken at mid-on. The complexion of the game had changed completely. The back of the Northants batting had been broken and the hundred had not been reached. The tail was long and the outcome of the match was very much in doubt.

Jim Yardley, a dour fighter, one of those stalwarts of county cricket who are the essence of the game and rarely receive the accolades, joined with Carter, the late inclusion, in a staunch and valuable stand. Yardley is a great sweeper and the shot was working well. He saw that Jack Simmons would have no more success — the old craftsman had bowled Lancashire back into the game by conceding only 17 runs in the twelve overs he bowled for the wickets of Williams and Lamb — and set about adding to the score.

The runs began to come with more ease and 150 had been reached when Yardley edged Reidy to Clive Lloyd at slip. Carter followed almost immediately, lbw to David Lloyd whose slow left-arm had replaced the inaccurate medium pace of O'Shaughnessy.

Sharp did not last long and, after a few brave blows, both Sarfraz and Mallender were back in the pavilion and the game was Lancashire's for the taking, for, at 174 for 9, thirteen runs

were needed for a Northants victory and the only man left to
help Tim Lamb get these runs was Jim Griffiths.

Of all the number elevens in first-class cricket, Jim Griffiths
must be the worst. While some give the impression of being
annoyed that they have been put so low in the batting order,
Jim Griffiths transmits the idea that his captain should have
declared earlier and saved him this embarrassment. His career
average for Northants is 2.92, his highest score 11, his run of
ducks formidable.

This was the man who was Northants' last hope.

When Griffiths came to the wicket there were eight overs left,
of which Holding and Allott could bowl two each. Lamb lectured
and advised Griffiths on several occasions. Tim Lamb, a thinking
cricketer, refused some easy singles to shield his partner from
the strike. There were flurries of leg-byes and Griffiths hit a
single. Holding and Allott were not held back for the last overs
but pitched into the attack. Holding, in particular, committed
the dreadful error of not forcing the batsman to play the ball.
The wicket-keeping was below standard and the fielding was
becoming excitable. And all this drama was being carried out in
a Stygian gloom, a half-light pervaded by the feverish enthusiasm
of the crowd who cheered every ball.

At the end of the fifty-ninth over the scores were level and
Tim Lamb consulted the umpires whom he sent hurrying off to
the scorers. There was a belief that one ball too few had been
bowled in the fifty-ninth over, but the query was as to the rules
of the competition. Both sides had the same score, both had
lost nine wickets. The scorers reported that Northants had the
faster scoring rate over the first thirty overs and therefore, if
Griffiths could survive the last over, to be bowled by David
Lloyd, then Northants would be the winners.

Four balls were bowled in an atmosphere of the utmost
tension. The fifth turned from leg, beat Griffiths and the
groping fingers of Fowler and the batsmen ran through for a
bye. Bats aloft, they continued their exultant run to the pavilion
as the crowds came to meet them.

Tim Lamb, whose contribution in every department of the
game had been immense, was named Man-of-the-Match. Jim
Griffiths treasured his 'one not out' as the innings of his career.

*   *   *

Further up the road, at Derby, the gloom and drizzle brought play to a close before a result could be reached.

Wood won the toss and asked Essex to bat on a wicket that was very green under skies that were heavy with cloud. There was no doubt that Wood's decision was the right one and he soon had wickets to prove it. There was an early stoppage through drizzle and then the left-arm swing of Tunnicliffe had Hardie caught behind. Derbyshire were ecstatic at the next wicket. Gooch was caught by Taylor diving in front of first slip and when Fletcher was yorked three runs later, the home side had taken an advantage which they should not let slip.

Much now depended on McEwan and, in company with Pont, he played with that easy charm which gives encouragement to Essex supporters and delight to all. The pair added fifty in twenty-one overs, valuable runs in these conditions, and their stand had stretched either side of lunch. It was the return of Hendrick and Newman in place of Steele and Wood that ended their partnership.

Hendrick made one rise sharply and Pont was caught behind. Two balls later came the greatest disaster of all for Essex when McEwan, who had looked in good form, played a ball to leg. He went for the quick single, rather unwisely, and Kim Barnett at mid-wicket picked up and threw down the stumps at the bowler's end in one movement, a superb piece of fielding.

Turner edged a Hendrick outswinger in the next over and Pringle, out of his depth with the bat, provided Taylor with his fifth catch behind the wicket.

Wood now attacked with his main bowling strength, gambling on bowling Essex out before the completion of the sixty overs. Norbert Phillip combated the assault well, curbing his natural tendency to hit at everything while still accumulating runs. Ray East gave dogged support until he was bowled by Newman with the score on 98.

David East had shown a tremendous zest for the game since forcing his way into the first team a few weeks earlier, winning the Man-of-the-Match award against Gloucestershire, and being very close to winning it at Hove. His batting had shown great resilience at Hove and that same quality was needed now.

He and Phillip defied the pace of Hendrick and Newman so that at 117 for 8 with six overs still remaining, the Derbyshire quicker bowlers had used their allocation of overs, and the last six overs would have to be bowled by Miller and Steele.

Phillip now launched his attack and the ball began to fly in all directions. Those last six overs produced 32 invaluable runs and, in all, Phillip and David East added 46 in ten overs.

Their partnership lasted until the final over of the innings, bowled by Geoff Miller. The off-spinner beat Phillip through the air and Taylor claimed his record sixth victim of the match. Phillip's innings had spanned twenty-five overs which, by his standards, was stagnation, but it represented a most courageous knock and one without which Essex would have been in a sorry predicament.

The last ball of the innings East hit mightily to long-off where Paul Newman, who had bowled so well, took a fine catch running round the boundary.

Derbyshire began their innings in the most miserable weather and the players soon left the field. On their return, in the fifth over of the innings, Wright, to his consternation, was lbw without playing a shot. His one run represented his best score against Essex in his last four innings for he had suffered the cruelty of being dismissed three times in twenty-four hours at Chelmsford without scoring.

Three overs and nine runs later, Peter Kirsten was also adjudged lbw and, as the drizzle descended again, Essex could at least sleep the night with a feeling that all was not lost.

As soon as Turner and Pringle took over the attack the following morning Derbyshire were struggling. Steele was bowled as he pushed forward and Turner moved the ball across Miller to hit the leg-stump.

The dependable Hill was bent on survival and his innings took on rock-like proportions as he remained not out at lunch. Immediately after the break, having batted for forty overs, he was out in ironic fashion for one who had played so resolutely. Barnett hit a ball from Pringle square on the off and Hill, contemplating a run, backed up so far that Fletcher's throw to the bowler beat him with ease.

Kim Barnett and Barry Wood now engaged in a vital stand of 51 in sixteen overs. Barnett is a young man of character whose place in the Derbyshire side was still uncertain. Vicious on anything that strayed to leg, he was beaten several times outside the off-stump but he never wavered in determination. Wood encouraged Barnett to look for the short singles and the wisdom and experience of the limited-over veteran gave the younger man's innings an added dimension.

Turner and Pringle, whose accuracy and relentlessness had made the Derbyshire task a difficult one, were seen off. Gooch bowled as well as he had done at Hove and only at the last was he in any way expensive.

Lever and Phillip were back for the final burst when Wood swung at the West Indian and was caught on the square-leg boundary. Seven runs later Barnett's fine innings came to an end when he injudiciously tried to clout Phillip through the off-side and the ball just clipped the wicket. Eighteen runs were needed off fifteen balls.

Much was hoped of Tunnicliffe, a powerful hitter on his day, but Lever bowled him with the first ball of the fifty-ninth over. This brought in Newman, whose fine bowling had been a feature of the Derbyshire challenge, and he and Taylor took six runs off the remaining five balls of Lever's over.

There was one over left. Eleven runs were needed for victory. In the pavilion sat Mike Hendrick, the last man in the order. Earlier in the day he had remained at home unwell, to be brought to the ground only if the situation so demanded. The situation had demanded and now only Newman and Taylor stood between him and sick-bed dash heroism.

So the last over began with Derbyshire needing eleven runs for victory. Bob Taylor with the strike. Norbert Phillip (3 for 32 in eleven overs) bowling.

Fletcher had his field flung wide. The boundaries were well guarded.

Taylor drove the first ball straight and the batsmen scampered two. The second delivery was run down to third man in the fashionable manner of the limited-over game and there was an easy single. Newman hooked the third ball hard to mid-on but there was only a single. The fourth ball was pushed square by Taylor for another single.

There was now the realisation that Derbyshire needed only five off the last two balls to give them victory, for five would bring the scores level and the home side would win on losing fewer wickets.

It was, of course, imperative that Newman should hit hard at the fifth ball of the over for the odds rested still with Essex. Poor Norbert Phillip who had performed so nobly for Essex in this match now bowled the worst of the seventy-two balls he bowled in the match. It was a long hop erring to leg which Newman pulled fiercely to the long leg boundary — and now Derbyshire needed one to win with one ball to be bowled.

There was a dramatic readjustment of the field as Fletcher pulled in his men to save the vital single.

The last ball of this match will remain frozen in the memory of all those who saw it and all those who played in the game. It will haunt the dreams of one man for the rest of his life.

Phillip bowled just short of a length, on or just outside the off-stump. Newman pushed forward and played the ball just past Fletcher in a silly mid-off position. Newman set off on an impossible run. Phillip, following through, picked up cleanly. Brian Hardie and others had taken up position at the bowler's end. A simple under-arm lob to Hardie and the bails would have been off and Newman would have been run out by yards. In that fraction of a second when all this should have been accomplished Norbert Phillip lost the sense of coolness that was essential to the moment. He wheeled towards the stumps and from a distance of not more than five yards he took a wild shy at them. He missed the wicket and all else. The Essex players sank to the ground in despair. Fletcher tried to console a dejected Phillip. For the third time in four years Essex had failed to reach the final of the sixty-over competition by losing more wickets than their opponents with the scores level.

Kim Barnett was named Man-of-the-Match and Derbyshire went off to Lord's to meet Northamptonshire in the final.

*   *   *

The weather was fine. The ground was full. Lord's was at its best, the pavilion rising from the turf in dominant benevolence.

None believed that the final could produce a match comparable in excitement to the two semi-finals. The early stages of the match supported this view.

Barry Wood won the toss and asked Northants to bat. There was a nervous, hesitant start for Derbyshire. The neatly academic

Taylor let through byes off the first delivery. Tunnicliffe was unable to strike a length and had to be removed from the attack after a couple of overs; the second over of the day produced 12 runs.

Larkins and Cook prospered. Wood tried to stem the flow of runs by bowling his own medium pace, and, in part, he was successful, greatly aided by the now polished wicket-keeping of Taylor standing up to the stumps. There was no containing the batsmen for long, however, and Larkins pulled Wood over square-leg for six and flicked Newman in the same direction for four. The boundaries were flowing with Larkins elegantly impressive and Cook practical and effective.

It seemed that Northants were in for a mighty score when, in the twenty-ninth over, Larkins pulled Wood again, high to square-leg, where Miller took a beautifully judged catch on the ropes. 99 for 1, the stage was set for Allan Lamb.

We expected an onslaught and the Derbyshire field to wilt, but the onslaught never came and the fielding strengthened in resolve and commitment.

For twelve overs Allan Lamb, considered by many to be the finest batsman playing in county cricket, fluttered and hesitated. Never once did he produce a shot worthy of his reputation and after facing forty deliveries he was run out when Miller's throw from extra cover hit the wicket. It was a very close thing.

The disappointment over Lamb, who had been promoted in the order to exploit a situation which it was felt would be so suited to his talents, was lessened somewhat by the blatantly positive Williams. He hit hard and it seemed that the expected onslaught would now be launched, but he was cut short just as his chunky figure had taken on the aura of belligerent permanence. He drove hard and high at Miller, operating from the Nursery End, and Alan Hill took a superb catch, falling to his left in front of the sight-screen.

Willey, back from injury, threatened for a time until he was wastefully run-out and the rest stuttered. Tunnicliffe returned to bowl splendidly, more than compensating for the sins of the morning.

With the air of lost direction around him, Cook reasserted Northants' authority by hitting Hendrick for three fours in one over to pass a fine hundred, an innings of composure and

positive application which won him the Man-of-the-Match
award and certainly influenced the selectors who chose him for
the tour of India. With his score on the Australian dread, 111,
he was lbw to Tunnicliffe.

There was none now who could strike the ball with enough
belief to provide the final impetus to the Northants innings. The
Derbyshire fielders retreated to the boundary in anticipation of
the final flourish, but it did not come. Mallender was caught
behind first ball and Hendrick, in many ways the least impressive
of the Derbyshire bowlers, took his only wicket with the last
ball of the innings when Tim Lamb swung wildly and was
bowled. 218 for 4 had become 235 for 9. It was a disappointing
total, but the opening stand of Cook and Larkins had insured
that it would be no easy score to make.

Certainly Derbyshire could be well pleased with their efforts,
but Hill and Wright faced a difficult time against Sarfraz and
Griffiths who swung the ball appreciably at the start of the
innings. Runs were scored, but survival and foundation were the
most important considerations.

Alan Hill applied himself with the determination born of a
professionalism which has weathered good times and bad. There
was some tentativeness, but there was resolution. The batsmen
survived the opening thrust without mishap. It was Mallender
who brought Northants success when Hill uncharacteristically
played across the line and was bowled. Fourteen runs in as
many overs does not sound a great score. Indeed, his contribution had been a minor one, but it had been vital.

Kirsten joined Wright in a stand which was crucial to Derbyshire's ambition of success. Their partnership could not match
the fluency of the Larkins—Cook stand earlier in the day, but it
was efficient in every detail and it provided the platform from
which an assault could be launched.

Kirsten saw this as no time for heroics. He consolidated and
accumulated rather than attempt the more brilliant shots in his
repertoire. Wright, at first watchful in the extreme, with nose
right over the ball, began to increase his range of strokes. Surely
there is no better player off the back foot. Leaning back on
his stumps, he thumped Sarfraz through the field either side of
the wicket with a majestic arrogance that denied argument.

With seventeen overs remaining Derbyshire were still one

hundred short of their target. In the next five overs 29 runs were scored, but Wright and Kirsten were dismissed.

In the forty-eighth over, bowled by Mallender from the Nursery End, Wright moved down the wicket and pulled the ball high into the tavern area for six. Two balls later he was lbw. Wood got off the mark with a single and then Kirsten, like Wright playing across the line, was also lbw. The game had swung back dramatically in favour of Northants.

There could not have been two better players for this crisis that now confronted Derbyshire than the two who had restored their position in the semi-final against Essex, Wood and Barnett. In five overs they added 24 runs before Sarfraz bowled Wood with a ball that moved in off the seam. Seven overs remaining, 47 needed.

It was not a situation for David Steele, his qualities lie in other directions. After three inglorious swats he was mercifully bowled playing a grotesque swipe at Griffiths.

Miller, the cricketer who has always suggested more than he has achieved and who had relinquished the captaincy only weeks before because it was having an adverse effect upon his form, immediately looked a man for the moment. He was busy and forceful, and he never lost poise or calm.

The fielding was now tense and eager. There were diving stops and Sarfraz fielded to his own bowling as if runs were donations to charity and he were Scrooge. The running between the wickets was electric.

The light is now fading rapidly and the fielders themselves have problems in sighting the ball as, all bar two, they are pushed back to the boundary ropes. Thirty-four runs are needed off four overs. A full toss from Sarfraz is deposited into the tavern by Miller with undisguised relish. Barnett is run out when going for a second run, a necessary gamble at this stage. Tunnicliffe is the next man in, an honest cricketer with ability to swing the ball as a bowler and, on occasions, to hit hard as a batsman. This proves to be such an occasion. In the fifty-ninth over of the innings, Sarfraz bowling, Tunnicliffe took two off the first ball, then hit a glorious square drive for four and followed it with a crashing drive back past the bowler to the pavilion rails. There was a single off the next ball and Derbyshire needed six off the last over to level the scores and win the match.

Miller took two off the first ball of Griffiths' over, the last of
the match, and a single from the next. Then there was a roar
that would usually signal a wicket as Tunnicliffe failed to score
off the third ball, but then there was a single and another single,
and we had arrived at the last ball of the match with one run
separating the scores.

Let us consider the actors in this drama. Bowling — Jim
Griffiths whose dogged batting, defying credibility, had made it
possible for Northants to be in this final when he had survived
and then run a bye off the penultimate ball of the semi-final
against Lancashire. Batting — Colin Tunnicliffe who had started
the game in some disarray with inaccurate overs and now found
himself cast as hero in the final act. Non-striker — Geoff Miller
who had passed from vice-captain of England to a figure in the
shadows within a period of a few months and now was thrust
suddenly back into the limelight.

Cook rearranged his field with great deliberation. Every
gesture and readjustment seemed to take an age. There is a
hubbub of excited and nervous chatter sweeping through the
entire crowd. The ball is back with Griffiths and suddenly all is
still. As he runs in every man and woman on the ground rises to
his or her feet. There is a roar of which you, unknowingly, are
a part. The ball pitches just outside leg-stump and Tunnicliffe
swings. It hits him on the pad and bounces out on the leg side.
Miller is charging down the wicket as Allan Lamb moves in from
mid-on and picks up and throws. Miller dives in the dust as the
ball hits the wicket and he is home! Tunnicliffe is safe at the
other end before anyone can retrieve the ball and throw to the
bowler's end. Miller stands with his arms in the air and waves his
bat in the exultation of success. Then he turns and he and
Tunnicliffe run to each other somewhere in the position of mid-
wicket and dance around the pitch clasped together as they are
engulfed in a sea of people.

NORTHAMPTONSHIRE *v* LANCASHIRE
NatWest Trophy Semi-Final
at Northampton
19 August 1981

Lancashire

A. Kennedy	c Yardley, b Sarfraz	6
* G. Fowler	c Sharp, b Williams	57
D. Lloyd	c Carter, b Williams	52
C.H. Lloyd (capt)	c Sharp, b T.M. Lamb	4
D.P. Hughes	c T.M. Lamb, b Sarfraz	13
B.W. Reidy	lbw, b T.M. Lamb	0
J. Abrahams	c Sharp, b T.M. Lamb	2
J. Simmons	not out	28
S.J. O'Shaughnessy	b Griffiths	3
P.J.W. Allott	lbw, b Griffiths	0
M.A. Holding	not out	12
Extras	lb 7, w 1, nb 1	9
	(for 9 wkts)	186

	O	M	R	W
Sarfraz	12	2	35	2
Griffiths	12	1	46	2
Mallender	12	3	28	—
T.M. Lamb	12	1	28	3
Williams	12	—	40	2

fall of wickets
1—6, 2—116, 3—123, 4—123, 5—123, 6—133, 7—144, 8—160, 9—161

Northamptonshire

G. Cook (capt)	b O'Shaughnessy	31
W. Larkins	lbw, b Allott	9
R.G. Williams	c C.H. Lloyd, b Simmons	41
A.J. Lamb	c D. Lloyd, b Simmons	10
T.J. Yardley	c C.H. Lloyd, b Reidy	31
R.M. Carter	lbw, b D. Lloyd	14
* G. Sharp	lbw, b Reidy	1
Sarfraz Nawaz	lbw, b Reidy	14
N.A. Mallender	c Fowler, b Allott	4
T.M. Lamb	not out	10
B.J. Griffiths	not out	1
Extras	b 2, lb 16, w 1, nb 2	21
	(for 9 wkts)	187

	O	M	R	W
Holding	12	2	36	—
Allott	12	2	32	2
O'Shaughnessy	4	—	25	1
Reidy	10	3	22	3
Simmons	12	4	17	2
D. Lloyd	9.5	—	34	1

fall of wickets
1—24, 2—58, 3—96, 4—97, 5—150, 6—152, 7—162, 8—170, 9—174

Northamptonshire won by 1 wicket

DERBYSHIRE *v* ESSEX
NatWest Trophy Semi-Final
at Derby
19 and 20 August 1981

Essex

B.R. Hardie	c Taylor, b Tunnicliffe	5
G.A. Gooch	c Taylor, b Newman	14
K.W.R. Fletcher (capt)	b Newman	4
K.S. McEwan	run out	28
K.R. Pont	c Taylor, b Hendrick	20
N. Phillip	st Taylor, b Miller	42
S. Turner	c Taylor, b Hendrick	0
D.R. Pringle	c Taylor, b Tunnicliffe	1
R.E. East	b Newman	6
*D.E. East	c Newman, b Miller	18
J.K. Lever	not out	4
Extras	lb 4, nb 3	7
		149

	O	M	R	W
Tunnicliffe	12	2	21	2
Hendrick	12	2	20	2
Newman	12	2	26	3
Wood	12	3	24	—
Steele	9	1	35	—
Miller	3	—	16	2

fall of wickets
1—19, 2—21, 3—24, 4—74, 5—75, 6—78, 7—90, 8—98, 9—144

Derbyshire

J.G. Wright	lbw, b Lever	1
A. Hill	run out	21
P.N. Kirsten	lbw, b Phillip	8
D.S. Steele	b Pringle	7
G. Miller	b Turner	0
K.J. Barnett	b Phillip	59
B. Wood (capt)	c R.E. East, b Phillip	18
* R.W. Taylor	not out	9
C.J. Tunnicliffe	b Lever	1
P.G. Newman	not out	7
M. Hendrick		
Extras	lb 12, w 3, nb 3	18
	(for 8 wkts)	149

	O	M	R	W
Lever	12	4	22	2
Phillip	12	2	42	3
Pringle	12	5	19	1
Turner	12	4	18	1
Gooch	12	2	30	—

fall of wickets
1—3, 2—12, 3—27, 4—30, 5—74, 6—125, 7—132, 8—133

Derbyshire won on losing fewer wickets with scores level

DERBYSHIRE *v* NORTHAMPTONSHIRE
NatWest Trophy Final
at Lord's
5 September 1981

Northamptonshire

G. Cook (capt)	lbw, b Tunnicliffe	111
W. Larkins	c Miller, b Wood	52
A.J. Lamb	run out	9
R.G. Williams	c Hill, b Miller	14
P. Willey	run out	19
T.J. Yardley	run out	4
* G. Sharp	c Kirsten, b Tunnicliffe	5
Sarfraz Nawaz	not out	3
N. A. Mallender	c Taylor, b Newman	0
T.M. Lamb	b Hendrick	4
B.J. Griffiths		
Extras	b 2, lb 9, w 1, nb 2	14
	(for 9 wkts)	235

	O	M	R	W
Hendrick	12	3	50	1
Tunnicliffe	12	1	42	2
Wood	12	2	35	1
Newman	12	—	37	1
Steele	5	—	31	—
Miller	7	—	26	1

fall of wickets
1—99, 2—137, 3—168, 4—204, 5—218, 6—225, 7—227, 8—227, 9—235

Derbyshire

A. Hill	b Mallender	14
J.G. Wright	lbw, b Mallender	76
P.N. Kirsten	lbw, b Mallender	63
B. Wood (capt)	b Sarfraz	10
K.J. Barnett	run out	19
D.S. Steele	b Griffiths	0
G. Miller	not out	22
C.J. Tunnicliffe	not out	15
* R.W. Taylor		
P.G. Newman		
M. Hendrick		
Extras	b 5, lb 7, w 3, nb 1	16
	(for 6 wkts)	235

	O	M	R	W
Sarfraz Nawaz	12	2	58	1
Griffiths	12	2	40	1
Mallender	10	1	35	3
Willey	12	—	33	—
T.M. Lamb	12	—	43	—
Williams	2	—	10	—

fall of wickets
1—41, 2—164, 3—165, 4—189, 5—191, 6—213

Derbyshire won on losing fewer wickets with scores level

INDIA *v* ZIMBABWE

PRUDENTIAL WORLD CUP

At Tunbridge Wells

18 June, 1983

There can be few lovelier cricket grounds in the world than the Nevill Ground at Tunbridge Wells. Enclosed by trees and banked by rhododendrons, it provides a bowl that focuses attention on cricket and the sun. For over a hundred years the Tunbridge Wells club has played there and a week of Kent cricket each season is an occasion not to be missed, but on Saturday, 18 June, 1983, the Nevill Ground provided an unlikely meeting place for the match between India and Zimbabwe.

When the schedule for the third world cup was drawn up a contest between India and Zimbabwe at Tunbridge Wells roused little enthusiasm. It was generally expected that by the time this fifth round match was reached, Australia and West Indies would have qualified for the semi-finals, and India and Zimbabwe would meet in a placid encounter before a handful of spectators, but Zimbabwe had beaten Australia on the first day of the tournament and the next day India had beaten West Indies so that both sides arrived at Tunbridge Wells with much at stake.

On a bright morning, with a little breeze, Kapil Dev won the toss and Gavaskar and Srikkanth went out to begin the Indian innings before a happily expectant crowd of about 3000 people.

Gavaskar, the hero of so many Tests for India, had been badly out of form and had been dropped for the previous match, but Vengsarkar had been injured against the West Indies and Gavaskar had been recalled. It was not a happy return. Rawson opened the bowling from the town end and his first ball lifted sharply and uncomfortably to cast immediate doubts in Gavaskar's mind as to the temperament of the wicket. These doubts were confirmed by the last ball of the over when Gavaskar essayed a limp leg-side shot at a ball that kept low and was l.b.w.

For India, there was worse to follow. Srikkanth played a maiden and they did not score a run until a leg-bye was recorded in the third over. In the fifth, having hit a boundary, Mohinder Amarnath edged Rawson to Houghton behind the stumps and India were 6 for 2. Srikkanth can be an exciting player, but his temperament is uncertain. Ignoring the responsibility that had been thrust upon him, he hit Curran high to mid-off where Butchart took a splendid running catch over his left shoulder. It was fine fielding, but it was insane batting.

Neither Patil nor Yashpal Sharma showed any signs of confidence or authority and in the tenth over Patil scooped at Curran and was caught behind on the leg-side. Kapil Dev immediately displayed a welcome positivity as he mixed purposeful defence with a willingness to punish the loose ball, but he had been at the wicket only three overs when he lost Yashpal Sharma who touched a ball outside the off-stump to Houghton. Thirteen overs gone and India were 17 for 5. The crowd had been shocked into almost total silence save for the jubilance of the small band of Zimbabwe supporters.

At last there was some relief for India as Roger Binny joined Kapil Dev in a sensible stand and 60 runs were added. For the first time it became apparent that there was a large contingent of Indian supporters on the ground. Rawson and Curran had been forced to rest and the bowling of Butchart and Fletcher presented fewer problems for the batsmen, but Traicos, the former South African Test off-spinner, produced a naggingly accurate spell which frustrated Binny and finally trapped him l.b.w. after 60 invaluable runs had been added. The worth of this stand was nullified in the next over when Shastri played a wretched shot and was caught at mid-off. India were 78 for 7 and Zimbabwe scented victory.

In the 36th over, Kapil Dev raised his own fifty and his team's hundred, but, lunching at 106 for 7, the Indians could not have been too happy.

It was in the period immediately after lunch that Kapil Dev asserted himself. In one over from Rawson, he hit 12 runs and with Madan Lal giving good support, 62 were added in 16 overs before Madan Lal gave Houghton his fourth catch of the day.

This was, in fact, Zimbabwe's last piece of joy. Kirmani, his head shaved, bristled with confidence and purpose, and Kapil Dev, having played himself in with mature sense, now began to hit the ball mightily to all parts of the ground. Suddenly one was aware that one was watching a very great innings. Often he hit in the air, but he hit with majesty and power that never suggested violence nor threatened to profane the beauty of the game or, indeed, of the venue. In the 49th over, he reached his century and, in the last eleven overs of the innings, he scored at the rate of seven runs an over.

Kirmani was a magnificent partner, running furiously, batting forcefully and elegantly and ever offering his captain the strike. In thirteen overs of brilliant batting, they added 100 runs. Zimbabwe's fielding, so good in the early stages of the innings, wilted in the sustained onslaught. India, 9 for 4 in the 10th over when Kapil Dev came to the wicket, closed on 266 for 8. The Indian captain had hit six 6's and sixteen 4's in his innings of 175 not out in 50 overs. It is the highest score ever recorded in a one-day international.

There could be nothing in the Zimbabwe innings to match this, it was felt, but Kapil Dev was tired and his opening overs were wayward. Paterson and Brown began briskly enough. It was sensible batting without too much colour or character, but a great deal of efficiency.

Roger Binny had replaced Kapil Dev and it was he who broke the stand when he had Paterson l.b.w. Heron was run out at the bowler's end in the next over after a scramble and a dive and 13 runs later, Andy Pycroft was caught behind off the turbaned Sandhu. Brown was stupidly run out, and with the backbone of the innings broken, it seemed that Zimbabwe would crumple.

Fletcher fell to a marvellous catch on the long-off boundary and Kevin Curran joined the pugnacious Houghton at 103 for 5. Much depended on Houghton who had had a good tournament, but Madan Lal beat him on the back foot and he was l.b.w.

There was now the general resignation to the fact that the game would meander quietly to its end, an end that had been shaped since Kapil Dev's arrival at the crease. Butchart and Curran added 55 and Peckover, in the unaccustomed number nine spot, hit a brisk 14, but when Rawson joined Curran at 189 for 8, the end was nigh. Curran now threw all caution to the wind. He savaged the medium pace bowling and, with a hint of desperation, Kapil Dev turned to an over of spin, but Shastri was hit for seven runs and quickly retired.

Rawson played the role of watchful support as Curran lashed the ball to all parts of the ground with tremendous power. At the end of the 55th over, Zimbabwe were 226 for 8. At the same stage, India had been 228 for 8. None now dared predict the outcome of this astonishing match, but in the 56th over, Curran played an uncharacteristically weak shot and was limply caught at mid-off. It was a meagre end to a brilliant piece of hitting.

It was just that on the last ball of the 57th over, Kapil Dev should catch and bowl Traicos to give his side victory, a victory which had been hard-earned in every respect and to which he had contributed so much. For those lucky enough to be at Tunbridge Wells that day, Kapil Dev's innings will remain long in the memory.

INDIA *v* ZIMBABWE
Prudential World Cup
at Tunbridge Wells
18 June, 1983

India

S.M. Gavaskar	lbw, b Rawson	0
K. Srikkanth	c Butchart, b Curran	0
M.B. Amarnath	c Houghton, b Rawson	5
S.M. Patil	c Houghton, b Curran	1
Yashpal Sharma	c Houghton, b Rawson	9
R.N. Kapil Dev (capt)	not out	175
R.M.H. Binny	lbw, b Traicos	22
R.J. Shastri	c Pycroft, b Fletcher	1
S. Madan Lal	c Houghton, b Curran	17
* S.M.H. Kirmani	not out	24
B.S. Sandhu		
	lb 9, w 3	12
	for 8 wickets	266

	O.	M.	R.	W.
Rawson	12	4	47	3
Curran	12	1	65	3
Butchart	12	2	38	—
Fletcher	12	2	59	1
Traicos	12	—	45	1

fall of wickets
1–0, 2–6, 3–6, 4–9, 5–17, 6–77, 7–78, 8–140

Zimbabwe

R.D. Brown	run out	35
G.A. Paterson	lbw, b Binny	23
J.G. Heron	run out	3
A.J. Pycroft	c Kirmani, b Sandhu	6
* D.L. Houghton	lbw, b Madan Lal	17
D.A.G. Fletcher (capt)	c Kapil Dev, b Amarnath	13
K.M. Curran	c Shastri, b Madan Lal	73
I.P. Butchart	b Binny	18
G.E. Peckover	c Yashpal Sharma, b Madan Lal	14
P.W.E. Rawson	not out	2
A.J. Traicos	c and b Kapil Dev	3
	lb 17, w 7, nb 4	28
		235

	O.	M.	R.	W.
Kapil Dev	11	1	32	1
Sandhu	11	2	44	1
Binny	11	2	45	2
Madan Lal	11	2	42	3
Amarnath	12	1	37	1
Shastri	1	–	7	–

fall of wickets
1–44, 2–48, 3–61, 4–86, 5–103, 6–113, 7–168, 8–189, 9–230

India won by 31 runs

INDIA *v* WEST INDIES

PRUDENTIAL WORLD CUP FINAL

At Lord's

25 June, 1983

Neither the first nor the second Prudential World Cup Finals had been disappointments. Each of them had been a memorable match although for different reasons. The third final was to be equally memorable and was to provide one of the most remarkable and unexpected results in the history of cricket.

From the start of the competition the West Indies had been firm favourites and India had been outsiders. That India had reached the final was an amazing feat. Before the tournament they had won 11 and lost 26 of the one-day internationals that they had played and of their 11 wins, 3 had been against Sri Lanka and one against East Africa. It was hardly a record that encouraged the belief that they would reach the world cup final. The West Indies were firm favourites and nothing that happened in the early part of the match detracted from the opinion that they would win handsomely, yet India, within the past week had come back from the depths of 17 for 5 to beat Zimbabwe and had then overwhelmed both Australia and England so that their confidence was high.

Clive Lloyd won the toss and followed his custom of asking the opposition to bat first. Roberts bowled first from the Nursery End and Garner opened from the Pavilion End. There was a relentless menace in the pace of the West Indian attack. Survival appeared to be the only possibility. Much depended upon Gavaskar, but, in the fifth over, with only two scored, he pushed indecisively at Roberts and was caught behind by Dujon.

Amarnath, the most reliable of India's batsmen in the competition, joined Srikkanth and was greeted by a bouncer from Garner, but he swayed gently away and settled to lay the foundation of India's innings. Srikkanth had been watchful and unaggressive, but now he unleashed a series of stunning shots.

If Srikkanth could sustain his bold, attacking, powerful cricket for more than an hour and a half, he would be the most exciting player that the game has ever known, but, like the moth, he flirts with danger, preferring the excitement of the moment to the boredom of longevity. He cut Garner ferociously over the slips for his first boundary. He drove Roberts to the mid-wicket boundary and, in the same over, hooked him over fine leg for 6. It was audacious batting. One square drive, down on one knee, was breathtaking in its explosive power.

Such joys do not last long, but we should cherish them while they are there. Off 57 balls he scored 38 exciting runs before falling to Marshall who looked to be an even greater menace than Roberts and Garner.

Amarnath and Yashpal Sharma moved into a more solid if less adventurous period and they gave hope of a substantial Indian total, but, with the score at 90 and lunch approaching, Amarnath was surprisingly bowled between bat and pad by Holding. Two runs later came a dreadful waste when Yashpal Sharma committed the indiscretion of trying to hit Gomes high over cover and failed to get to the pitch of the ball so that Logie, fielding for Haynes who had hurt his hand, took a simple catch. Once more Lloyd had used the tactic of employing his weakest bowler just before lunch so challenging India to score at a time when they wanted to contain. Once more the ploy had proved successful.

After lunch, Kapil Dev played two fine shots off Gomes, but, in attempting to hit a six, he was caught at long-on. There was dejection in the Indian camp for with him, surely, had gone India's last hopes of making a winning score. In the next over, Kirti Azad was caught at square-leg and in the 36th over, Binny went the same way. 130 for 7, and five wickets had fallen in 7 overs for 40 runs. All predictions as to a one-sided contest were coming true. Madan Lal, Kirmani, Patil and Sandhu all scored useful runs which mocked the efforts of some of the earlier batsmen. Sandhu was hit on the head by a Marshall bouncer but batted courageously as the last wicket added 22, but India failed to last their quota of overs, and the only question seemed to be at what time and by how many wickets would West Indies win.

When Haynes crashed Sandhu through extra-cover for 4 it appeared that West Indies would win sooner than later, but then came a shock. Sandhu was bowling from the Nursery End. He pitched a ball outside Greenidge's off-stump and the batsman lifted his bat to let the ball pass by, but it moved back at him and knocked his stumps over. This brought in Richards. He walked to the wicket with an air of arrogance and disdain. He translated that air into physical terms when he pulled Sandhu to mid-wicket for 4. Kapil Dev was driven through mid-off and mid-wicket for further boundaries.

Madan Lal came on at the Nursery End and Richards hit him for three 4's in his first over. West Indies were racing to victory.

In Madan Lal's next over, however, Haynes drove loosely and was caught at extra cover. Clive Lloyd came in to an emotional reception. He had indicated that he might well give up the captaincy and that his days in international cricket were drawing to a close. He had not been fully fit during the season and when he went for his opening single he pulled a muscle and Haynes reappeared as runner.

In Madan Lal's next over, the 14th, Richards swung the ball contemptuously and high over mid-wicket. There was a roar of approval from West Indian supporters at another great hit, but the ball hovered and sprinting back, Kapil Dev took a splendid catch. For West Indies this was the moment of truth.

The Indians had never lost heart, but now their play took on a new urgency. Again Madan Lal moved in from the Nursery End. His away swinger found the edge of Gomes' bat and Gavaskar held on to a smart catch at slip. Immediately, Lloyd attempted to thump Binny through the covers, but, instead, he hit the ball straight into the hands of mid-off.

At tea, West Indies were 76 for 5 from 25 overs, and the game had changed completely in the space of a quarter of an hour. The determined bowling of Madan Lal, accurate and intelligent and deceptive in movement, had raised hope where none had seemed to exist.

The interval, it was thought, would restore some sanity to the West Indian batting. They needed only 108 to win in 35 overs, and there was still the batting available to make these runs. If advice and consultation had taken place, Bacchus could not have heard it, for in the first over after tea, he chased a widish delivery from Sandhu who had returned at the Nursery End and Kirmani took a catch as brilliant and spectacular as it was important. Now the unthinkable had become probable.

There followed a period of great tension as Dujon and Marshall batted sensibly for the run-rate required was still little more than three an over and 43 runs were added without fuss. Madan Lal's glorious spell was now at an end and Kapil Dev's options were becoming fewer. He brought on Amarnath at the Nursery End. His first ball was a gentle loosener and Dujon responded by dropping it down just as gently onto his stumps.

65 runs were needed from 18 overs with three wickets in hand, but five runs later an innocent looking seamer from Amarnath moved a fraction and Gavaskar clung on to the chance at slip.

Kapil Dev returned for the final onslaught and he had Roberts l.b.w. 126 for 9 and only Garner and Holding standing between India and a famous victory.

The last pair stood firm against Kapil Dev and the score edged closer to the target, but then Amarnath beat Holding's shuffle and hit him on the pads. Umpire Bird's finger went up and India were champions of the world.

The crowd swarmed onto the field and the Indian players galloped off in undisguised joy. It was the greatest day in the history of Indian cricket. It was also a day to savour, a monument for the greatest of games.

INDIA *v* WEST INDIES
Prudential World Cup Final
at Lord's
25 June, 1983

India

S.M. Gavaskar	c Dujon, b Roberts	2
K. Srikkanth	lbw, b Marshall	38
M.B. Amarnath	b Holding	26
Yashpal Sharma	c sub (Logie), b Gomes	11
S.M. Patil	c Gomes, b Garner	27
R.N. Kapil Dev (capt)	c Holding, b Gomes	15
Kirti Azad	c Garner, b Roberts	0
R.M.H. Binny	c Garner, b Roberts	2
S. Madan Lal	b Marshall	17
* S.M.H. Kirmani	b Holding	14
B.S. Sandhu	not out	11
	B 5, lb 5, w 9, nb 1	20
		183

	O.	M.	R.	W.
Roberts	10	3	32	3
Garner	12	4	24	1
Marshall	11	1	24	2
Holding	9.4	2	26	2
Gomes	11	1	49	2
Richards	1	—	8	—

fall of wickets
1–2, 2–59, 3–90, 4–92, 5–110, 6–111, 7–130, 8–153, 9–161

West Indies

C.G. Greenidge	b Sandhu	1
D.L. Haynes	c Binny, b Madan Lal	13
I.V.A. Richards	c Kapil Dev, b Madan Lal	33
C.H. Lloyd (capt)	c Kapil Dev, b Binny	8
H.A. Gomes	c Gavaskar, b Madan Lal	5
S.F.A. Bacchus	c Kirmani, b Sandhu	8
* P.J. Dujon	b Amarnath	25
M.D. Marshall	c Gavaskar, b Amarnath	18
A.M.E. Roberts	lbw, b Kapil Dev	4
J. Garner	not out	5
M.A. Holding	lbw, b Amarnath	6
	B 4, w 10	14
		140

	O.	M.	R.	W.
Kapil Dev	11	4	21	1
Sandhu	9	1	32	2
Madan Lal	12	2	31	3
Binny	10	1	23	1
Amarnath	7	—	12	3
Kirti Azad	3	—	7	—

fall of wickets
1–5, 2–50, 3–57, 4–66, 5–66, 6–76, 7–119, 8–124, 9–126

India won by 43 runs

MIDDLESEX *v* ESSEX

BENSON AND HEDGES CUP FINAL
At Lord's
23 July, 1983

For the first time in the history of either of the knock-out competitions the two best teams in the country reached the final when Middlesex, leading in the Schweppes County Championship, and Essex, pressing them close and eventually to overtake them, met in the Benson and Hedges Final at Lord's in 1983.

On the eve of the match both sides had been troubled by injuries. Middlesex lost Roland Butcher who had been hit in the face by a ball from Ferris in the match against Leicestershire and Essex were concerned about John Lever who had undergone surgery for a stomach abcess only a week before the final. Lever declared himself fit to play, but whether this was a wise decision or not is open to question. In the event, Norbert Phillip was left out from the side which had suffered an amazing defeat at the hands of Kent in the NatWest Trophy only three days previously, and Tomlins won Butcher's place in the Middlesex side.

In the days before the final, the weather had been glorious, but the Saturday broke with a disappointing drizzle. Fletcher won the toss and after much deliberation and consultation with Gooch and Lever, he asked Middlesex to bat. Play began fifty minutes after the scheduled time, in steaming damp.

Barlow began confidently, crashing Lever through the offside for four three times in the bowler's first two overs and so raising doubts as to Lever's fitness. But the doubts were soon transferred to Middlesex.

Foster had bowled very quickly in his first over. The smooth run, the positive and aggressive approach allied to the high and handsome delivery all breathed menace. In the fourth over of the innings, Slack edged a very fast delivery to slip where Gooch took a mighty right-handed catch low down. It was match-winning bowling and catching and Middlesex were 10 for 1.

Radley, the workman, joined Barlow and began an innings which was to last 56 overs. Most of the time he was to spend on the front foot and he was to save his side from total collapse, ultimately claiming the Gold Award. In the tenth over, he lost Barlow. The left-hander had just hit Foster for 2 to mid-off, but the next ball was again very fast and moved back at the batsman to knock over his middle stump. It was fine bowling.

Now came the Middlesex hope, skipper Mike Gatting. Foster and Lever were replaced after bowling seven overs each and putting Essex firmly in control. That control was momentarily threatened when Pringle bowled two ineffective overs lacking in pace and accuracy. Troubled by a recent spate of no-balls, he appeared hesitant in his run to the wicket, and he was replaced by Gooch as Turner's partner.

The spell of bowling that we now witnessed from the two medium pacers should have won the match for Essex for rarely can two players have bowled better in a vital match at Lord's. Turner bowled from the Nursery End and, seam up, maintained a frustrating length which, with Gooch, in similar pattern and achieving comparable movement, threatened to suffocate Middlesex to the point of extinction. By the 29th over, the score was only 72. Gatting turned Gooch to the Mound Stand square-leg boundary. Foster set off in pursuit and stopped the ball inches from the line as Gatting scampered for an improbable third run. Foster swooped, picked up, turned and threw all in one movement. The ball was straight over the top of the stumps where David East collected and broke the wicket with a flourish as Gatting dived despairingly for the crease. Tomlins was l.b.w. first ball and Middlesex were 74 for 4.

Turner's splendidly economic spell ended with the 36th over. His eleven overs had cost only 24 runs and Middlesex were still seven short of the hundred. Emburey was struggling agonisingly to put bat to ball, but Radley soldiered on, pushing here, nudging there, crouching lower and lower and presenting a symbol of defiance.

There followed a series of events which, on reflection, were to prove decisive in determining the outcome of the match. Emburey was dropped by Fletcher at mid-off and shortly after, in the 40th over, Radley reached his fifty. Emburey survived Gooch's magnificent spell, but he perished in the 44th over when he attempted to drive Lever, now bowling from the

Nursery End, and skied the ball in the slip area where David East moved across to take the catch. Significantly though, in the over before this, Radley, on 59, had been dropped by Pont.

These lapses gave Middlesex the respite that they needed and Radley was able to cajole Downton, Edmonds, Williams and Daniel to help him add 73 from the last 11 overs. Pringle and Lever were the main sufferers, and here Essex judgement was questioned. Lever was obviously far from fit and once Pringle had erred, it was difficult to understand why Ray East had been chosen if he was not to bowl, nor why Phillip had been omitted. Nevertheless, Essex had generally bowled and fielded well and 196, though better than expected earlier, looked an insignificant total.

This view was quickly confirmed. Hardie crashed Daniel through the covers in the opening over, and the second over, for Cowans and for Middlesex, was traumatic.

Gatting set an attacking off-side field. Cowans bowled short. Three times Gooch bludgeoned him to leg for 4, twice he hit him for 2. They were shots of great majesty and Lord's shook to them.

After two overs Cowans was replaced by Williams who was immediately driven wide of mid-on for another boundary. In the 8th over Williams bowled a no-ball which brought up the fifty. After ten overs, Essex were 71 for 0 with Gooch on 40 and Hardie on 25. It was thrilling stuff.

Williams moved in to bowl the 12th over. Gooch hit him straight and imperious to the Nursery End sight-screen. The next ball he again aimed to drive, but he edged and Downton took the catch very low down. 79 for 1 at six and a half an over.

The 13th over of the innings was the first maiden. McEwan, troubled by an injured wrist, was finding it hard to settle into a rhythm, and the run rate dropped as Hardie ceased to hit the ball with his earlier confidence. Edmonds had applied the break, but, at tea, off 25 overs, Essex were 113 for 1, Hardie 34, McEwan 26, and victory seemed a formality.

Five overs after tea, McEwan drove Edmonds low to Williams at mid-off where the fielder swooped and claimed a catch, a claim which the umpire upheld.

Eight runs came in the next two overs, four of them were

extras. Fletcher dithered and prodding forward at Edmonds who bowled from the Nursery End, he was taken at silly mid-off, bat-pad. Hardie had scored only 13 in the past 20 overs, but Essex needed only 61 for victory with 7 wickets in hand and 23 overs in which to get them.

Pont was dropped by Cowans in the 35th over, but he was less fortunate three overs later. The 150 had just been passed and Williams was operating from the Nursery End. He bowled a bouncer which Pont took on the side of the helmet. Evidently the impact pressed a helmet stud into the temple and Pont, stunned, recoiled and dropped his bat. In doing so, he dislodged the off bail and was out, hit wicket. Essex needed 46 from 17 overs with six wickets in hand.

Hardie had remained flat-footed against Edmonds and Emburey. He was totally becalmed. After the departure of Gooch he had virtually ceased to bat. In the 41st over, perhaps in desperation, he flashed at Cowans, who had returned at the Pavilion End, and was caught behind. His 22 runs since Gooch's departure had occupied 29 overs. In 16 overs since tea, he had scored 15 runs.

Turner and Pringle now found themselves faced by an enemy who, under the inspiring leadership of a captain who refused to admit defeat, had refound self-belief. Emburey had induced strokelessness, and Gatting supported his bowlers with attacking fields rarely seen in the one-day game. Pringle and Turner nudged, ran and showed good sense and temperament. Runs did not come as quickly as they had done at the start, but in 9 overs, they added 24 runs and at the end of the 50th over, Essex stood only 17 short of victory and five batsmen still remained to be dismissed.

Pringle had managed two refreshing 4's and Turner one when, with the first ball of the 52nd over, Daniel had Pringle l.b.w. Twelve were needed off 23 balls.

David East managed one and there was a leg-bye but Turner, who had chosen to survive Emburey when he might have hit, now chose to hit at Cowans in the gathering gloom. He clouted him high to deep mid-on where John Carr, fielding as substitute for Williams, took a fine catch.

David East touched a ball down the leg-side to the fine-leg boundary and Essex were 191 for 7, six needed and more than two overs in which to get them. Next ball East tried to hit over mid-wicket for what would have been a crucial four. Gatting leapt and just got a hand to the ball, breaking its speed. Spinning round, he caught it as it dropped behind him. It was a splendid catch by a fine cricketer who, within the space of a few months, had established himself as a very fine captain.

We now had Ray East and Neil Foster together. This was to be Foster's only limited-over match innings of the season, and Ray East, as he had proved before, was temperamentally not at his best in a situation such as this. Daniel bowled a wide — 192 for 8. On the fifth ball of the over, Ray East was struck on the pad and as the ball squirted out on the off side, he charged up the wicket in search of an impossible leg-bye. Before he could regain his ground, Radley had thrown down the wicket from point.

Lever played out the last ball of the over and so left five runs needed from the final over. With his first ball, Norman Cowans yorked Foster and Middlesex had won a famous victory.

Foster, for whom the game had held so much earlier in the day, stood forlornly at the crease as the crowd swept on to the field. Gatting, a master of tactics, had snatched a victory when none seemed possible. Cowans, ravaged by Gooch, had come back to take three wickets in his last four deliveries. Essex, many of their players close to tears, had suffered a second shattering defeat inside four days. But in the Stygian gloom of Lord's at 8.50 on a July evening, spectators sank back in exhaustion at the great match that they had witnessed.

MIDDLESEX *v* ESSEX
Benson and Hedges Cup Final
at Lord's
23 July, 1983

Middlesex

G.D. Barlow	b Foster	14
W.N. Slack	c Gooch, b Foster	1
C.T. Radley	not out	89
M.W. Gatting (capt)	run out	22
K.P. Tomlins	lbw, b Gooch	0
J.E. Emburey	c D.E. East, b Lever	17
* P.R. Downton	c Fletcher, b Foster	10
P.H. Edmonds	b Pringle	9
N.F. Williams	c and b Pringle	13
W.W. Daniel	not out	2
N.G. Cowans		
	B 3, lb 9, w 4, nb 3	19
	for 8 wickets	196

	O.	M.	R.	W.
Lever	11	1	52	1
Foster	11	2	26	3
Pringle	11	–	54	2
Turner	11	2	24	–
Gooch	11	2	21	1

fall of wickets
1–10, 2–25, 3–74, 4–74, 5–123, 6–141, 7–171, 8–191

Essex

G.A. Gooch	c Downton, b Gooch	46
B.R. Hardie	c Downton, b Cowans	49
K.S. McEwan	c Cowans, b Edmonds	34
K.W.R. Fletcher (capt)	c Radley, b Edmonds	3
K.R. Pont	hit wkt, b Williams	7
D.R. Pringle	lbw, b Daniel	16
S. Turner	c sub (Carr), b Cowans	9
* D.E. East	c Gatting, b Cowans	5
R.E. East	run out	0
N.A. Foster	b Cowans	0
J.K. Lever	not out	0
	lb 12, w 3, nb 8	23
		192

	O.	M.	R.	W.
Daniel	11	2	34	1
Cowans	10.1	–	39	4
Williams	11	–	45	2
Emburey	11	3	17	–
Edmonds	11	3	34	2

fall of wickets
1–79, 2–127, 3–135, 4–151, 5–156, 6–185, 7–187, 8–191, 9–192

Middlesex won by 4 runs